DESIGN IDEAS for

Kitchens

CREATIVE
HOMEOWNER®

DESIGN IDEAS for Kitchens

Susan Hillstrom

CREATIVE HOMEOWNER®, Upper Saddle River, New Jersey

CREATIVE
HOMEOWNER®

A Division of Federal Marketing Corp.
Upper Saddle River, NJ

DESIGN IDEAS FOR KITCHENS

SENIOR EDITOR	Kathie Robitz
EDITOR	Lisa Kahn
SENIOR GRAPHIC DESIGN COORDINATOR	Glee Barre
PHOTO COORDINATOR	Mary Dolan
JUNIOR EDITOR	Jennifer Calvert
DIGITAL IMAGING SPECIALIST	Frank Dyer
INDEXER	Schroeder Indexing Services
COVER DESIGN	Glee Barre
FRONT COVER PHOTOGRAPHY	(clockwise from left) Olson Photography, LLC; courtesy of Sub-Zero; courtesy of Vetrazzo, photographer: Joel Puliatti ©2008; Eric Roth; courtesy of Kohler; courtesy of Plain & Fancy
BACK COVER PHOTOGRAPHY	(top) Tony Giammarino, Giammarino & Dworkin; (bottom) Eric Roth

CREATIVE HOMEOWNER

VICE PRESIDENT AND PUBLISHER	Timothy O. Bakke
MANAGING EDITOR	Fran J. Donegan
ART DIRECTOR	David Geer
PRODUCTION COORDINATOR	Sara M. Markowitz

Current Printing (last digit)
10 9 8 7 6 5 4 3 2 1

Design Ideas for Kitchens, 2nd Edition
Library of Congress Control Number: 2008934563
ISBN-10: 1-58011-438-5
ISBN-13: 978-1-58011-438-7

Manufactured in the United States of America

CREATIVE HOMEOWNER®
A Division of Federal Marketing Corp.
24 Park Way
Upper Saddle River, NJ 07458
www.creativehomeowner.com

GREEN EDITION

Planet Friendly Publishing
✔ Made in the United States
✔ Printed on Recycled Paper
Learn more at www.greenedition.org

At Creative Homeowner we're committed to producing books in an earth-friendly manner and to helping our customers make greener choices.

Manufacturing books in the United States ensures compliance with strict environmental laws and eliminates the need for international freight shipping, a major contributor to global air pollution.

Printing on recycled paper also helps minimize our consumption of trees, water, and fossil fuels. *Design Ideas for Kitchens* was printed on paper made with 10% post-consumer waste. According to Environmental Defense's Paper Calculator, by using this innovative paper instead of conventional papers, we achieved the following environmental benefits:

Trees Saved: 65

Water Saved: 23,749 gallons

Solid Waste Eliminated: 3,929 pounds

Air Emissions Eliminated: 7,244 pounds

For more information on our environmental practices, please visit us online at www.creativehomeowner.com/green

Dedication

To my father, Vilas J. Boyle, who got me started.

Contents

Introduction

Ever since people gathered around fires in caves, the place where food is prepared has been designated as the heart of the home. Technological advances have made the kitchen of today a marvel of efficiency, but it still retains a primal appeal—it's the place that draws people together. Everyone wants to linger in the kitchen, especially with others—members of the household, extended family, friends, neighbors, pets. As the experts are fond of saying, the modern kitchen is a "multipurpose room." More than just a job site for cooking and cleaning up, it's also the living room, dining room, family room, and the home office all in one. Therefore, the creation of a kitchen is a complicated affair. You can't just move a rock closer to the fire—you need to define your taste and juggle cabinets, appliances, countertops, and lighting to create a room that meets your cooking and socializing needs, expresses your design sensibilities, and fits within your budget. That's where *Design Ideas for Kitchens* comes in handy. Use it as a guide through the planning and designing process. Let the beautiful photographs and helpful information alert you to the latest kitchen trends and products—and inspire you with a wealth of possibilities.

LEFT The simple design of this family kitchen allows the quality of the materials to speak for themselves.

TOP Hundreds of new options abound for customizing your kitchen's design, layout, and functionality.

BELOW Reinvented appliances—such as this fridge in a drawer—allow everyone to get more out of the kitchen.

1

Begin with the Basics

No longer tucked away and closed off from the rest of the house, today's kitchen is a front-and-center space where family and friends gather to cook, eat, and entertain. Efficiency is important, of course, but the modern kitchen has to look great, too. With some effort, and perhaps help from a professional, your new or remodeled kitchen can be everything you want it to be—a warm and welcoming room where you prepare meals efficiently, spend time with your family, sit quietly with a cup of coffee, and entertain in style.

- designed for living
- kitchen layouts
- islands and peninsulas
- eat-in kitchens

This urban kitchen, with its abundant square footage and ample natural light, has style, function, and storage to spare.

LEFT Eco-friendly bamboo cabinetry paired with copper countertops and backsplashes make a bold design statement in this contemporary kitchen.

BELOW LEFT A stainless-steel refrigerator fits seamlessly into the custom-built cabinetry, planned for maximum storage and display.

OPPOSITE, TOP AND BOTTOM Collectibles take center stage in the large glass-fronted cabinet; the kitchen's copper surfaces have natural antibacterial properties.

designed for living

Your dream kitchen will take some planning to meet the needs of your household. Find your focus in a family conference, discussing the new kitchen from each person's point of view. First, look at the kitchen you've got. What's good about it? What's not so good? Is it too small, too dark? Is storage lacking? Are the appliances old, the finishes faded? Have you always hated the cabinets?

Next, focus on the future. How will each family member use the new kitchen? Will everyone cook? Is this where the kids will hang out with their friends or do homework? Will you want a baking center, planning desk, dining area? Do you love to entertain? How sociable do you actually want to be? Will you chat with guests while you cook, or do you want to prepare your culinary masterpieces in private? Will you want to open your new kitchen to surrounding rooms or to the outdoors?

What about the size? Can you expand your present kitchen by annexing nearby space, thus avoiding major structural changes? Does your budget permit an addition? Perhaps just reconfiguring your present kitchen will do the trick.

Your family conference will produce a clear picture of the kitchen your family wants. Put the ideas you've discussed on paper in the form of a rough sketch. Whether you do the work yourself or turn the sketch over to a professional, you'll have taken the first step toward making your kitchen dreams a reality.

family-friendly functionality

The U-shaped family kitchen shown here is filled with the latest design innovations yet is still warm and inviting. "Green" products include halogen lighting, formaldehyde-free cabinets, and recycled paper countertops.

sliding board

This bamboo cutting board fits snugly over the counter yet can be moved as needed.

OPPOSITE TOP While spacious, the kitchen is arranged in tight and efficient work zones.

ABOVE Light green, charcoal, stainless steel, and natural wood make a pleasing color combination.

RIGHT Dishes and glassware displayed on open shelving lend the kitchen a homey, country-style appeal.

LEFT Every inch of this urban galley kitchen is smartly designed to maximize storage, minimize clutter, and enhance usable space.

RIGHT Built-in storage options include floor-to-ceiling cabinets, shelving, and large drawers under the cooktop, wall ovens, and curved counter.

BELOW In the baking prep area, appliances, ingredients, and other essentials are neatly concealed behind metal tambour doors that roll up and down with ease.

OPPOSITE BOTTOM Open areas under the sink and opposite wall create a sense of airiness in the narrow center aisle.

Go Green

Eco-friendly materials are available in an ever-growing range of styles and costs. Look for "green" countertops made of recycled tile, quartz composite—even paper or hemp.

parking spot

Every kitchen needs a comfortable chair or window seat where the cook can relax for a bit.

design pros

- **Architects** plan, design, and oversee new construction and major remodels. You will need one if your kitchen project involves an addition or an extensive makeover of existing space.
- **Certified Kitchen Designers (CKDs)** are schooled in all aspects of kitchen design, from layouts to equipment and materials to wiring and plumbing. Before choosing one, make sure your design sensibilities mesh.
- **Interior designers** can be of great help in the selection of materials and the creation of a visually appealing room. Not all are adept at kitchen design, so be sure to ask about a potential candidate's expertise in this field.
- **General contractors** usually work from plans drawn up by another professional. They will get permits, install cabinets, and oversee the work of electricians and other tradespersons. Some specialize in kitchens and work in partnership with designers.

kitchen layouts

available space and budget will dictate the size of your new kitchen. But you can establish an efficient layout no matter what the dimensions if you employ the work triangle—that is, place the range, refrigerator, and sink so they form the three points of a triangle and are no less than 4 and no more than 9 feet apart. Less space between the elements makes the work space too cramped; more space wastes steps, time, and energy. Traditionally, all of the layouts considered most efficient by kitchen experts were based on this work triangle. However, as kitchens have become multifunctional, new configurations may feature two or more work zones or activity centers. Choose the shape that best suits the space you have and the way you want to use it.

one-wall kitchens locate cabinets,

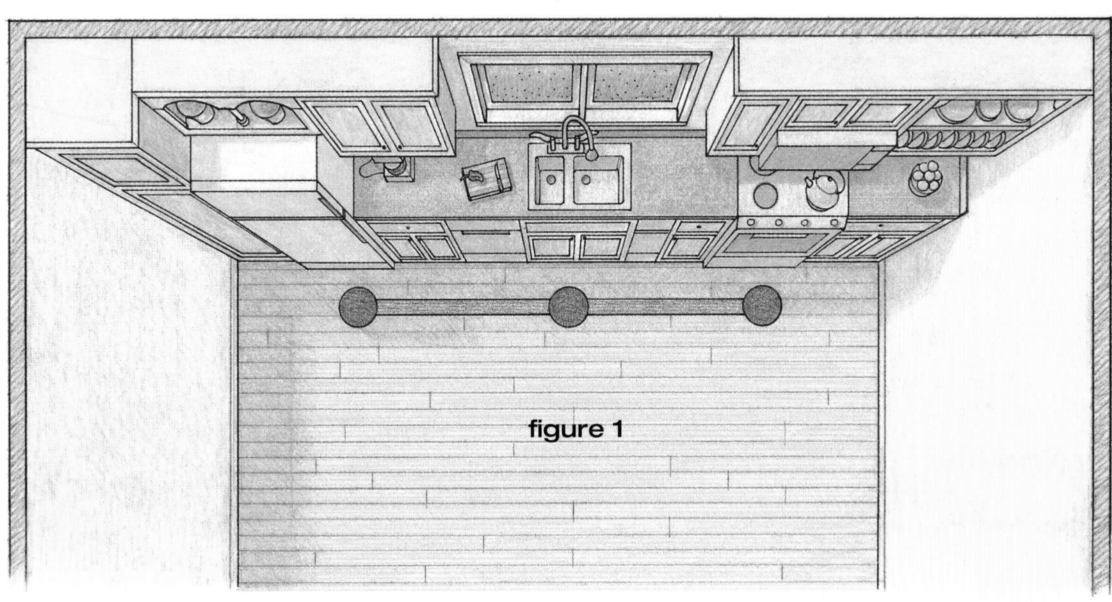

counters, and appliances against a single wall

OPPOSITE Although most of this kitchen is arranged against one wall, an ample island with an extra sink creates room for a second cook.

FIGURE 1 A typical one-wall kitchen arrangement

FIGURE 2 Adding a peninsula or extending a line of cabinets creates a more efficient L.

FIGURE 3 If space permits, a cooktop can be located in an island, as shown.

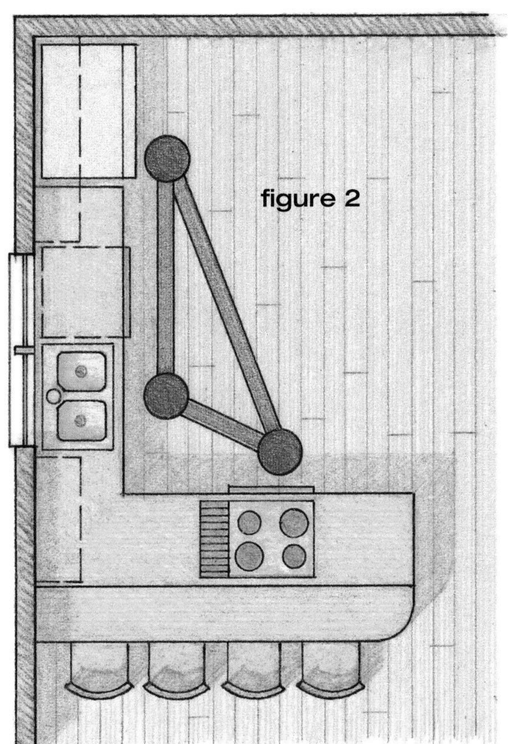

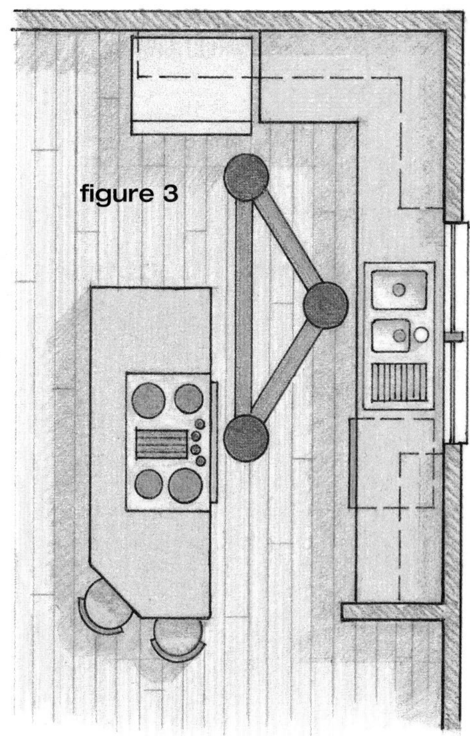

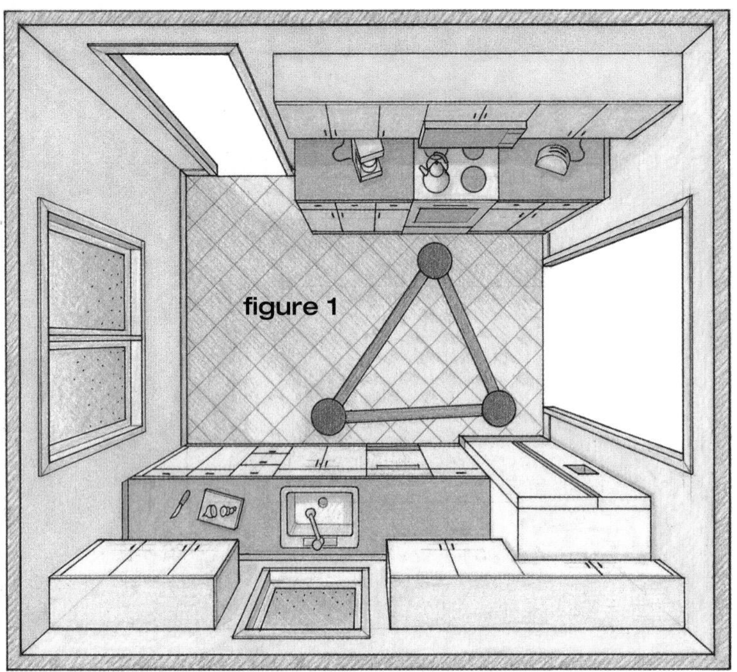

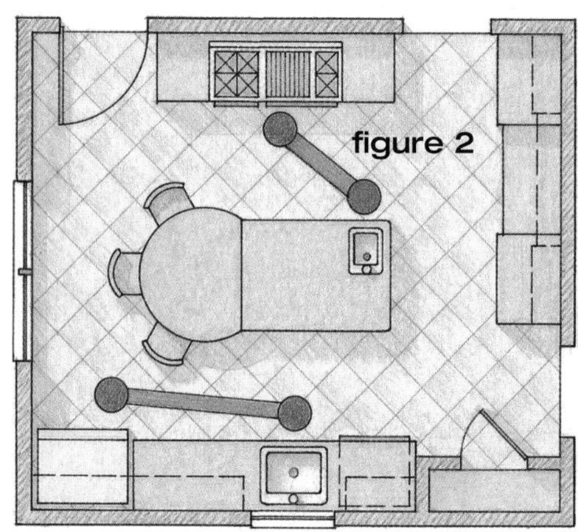

how a galley kitchen works

RIGHT A galley kitchen places cabinets, counters, and appliances on opposite walls. Modest dimensions don't have to compromise efficiency when essentials are within easy reach of the cook.

FIGURE 1 A typical galley kitchen

FIGURE 2 If space permits, create a secondary work zone or an eating area with an island.

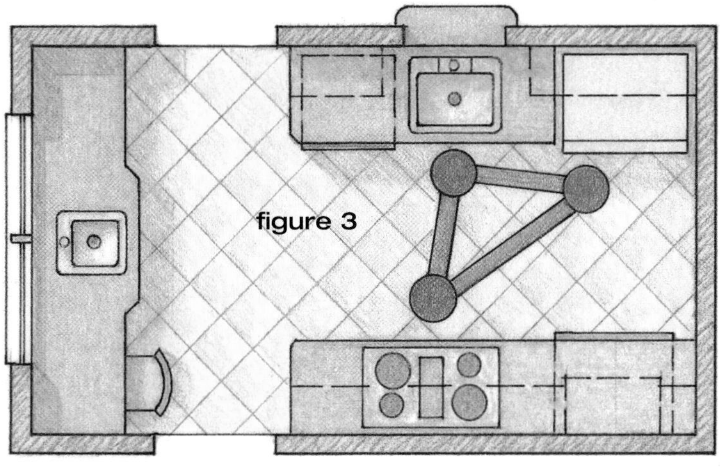

ABOVE Smart planning leaves space for a nearby eating area.

FIGURE 3 If possible, locate entryways outside the work zone.

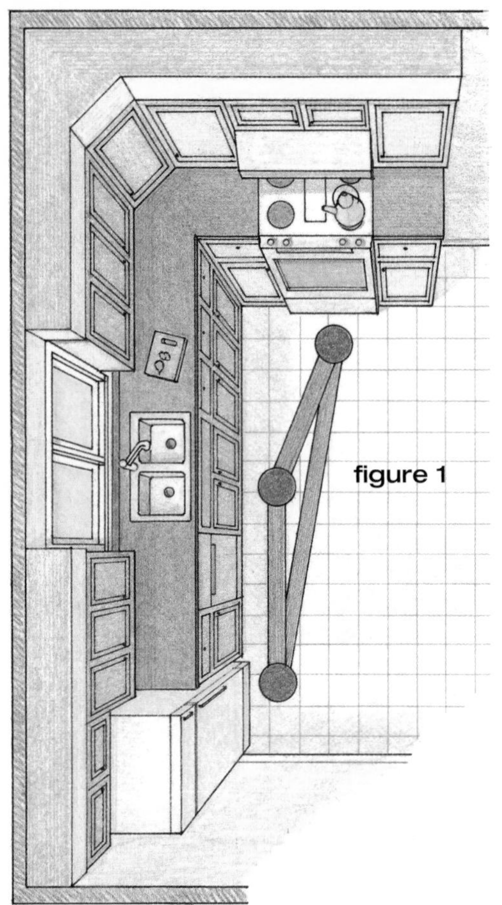

an L-shaped layout offers more counter space

FIGURE 1
A typical L-shaped arrangement

FIGURE 2
Installing a curved island diagonally across from an L configuration expands the possibilities of the work triangle.

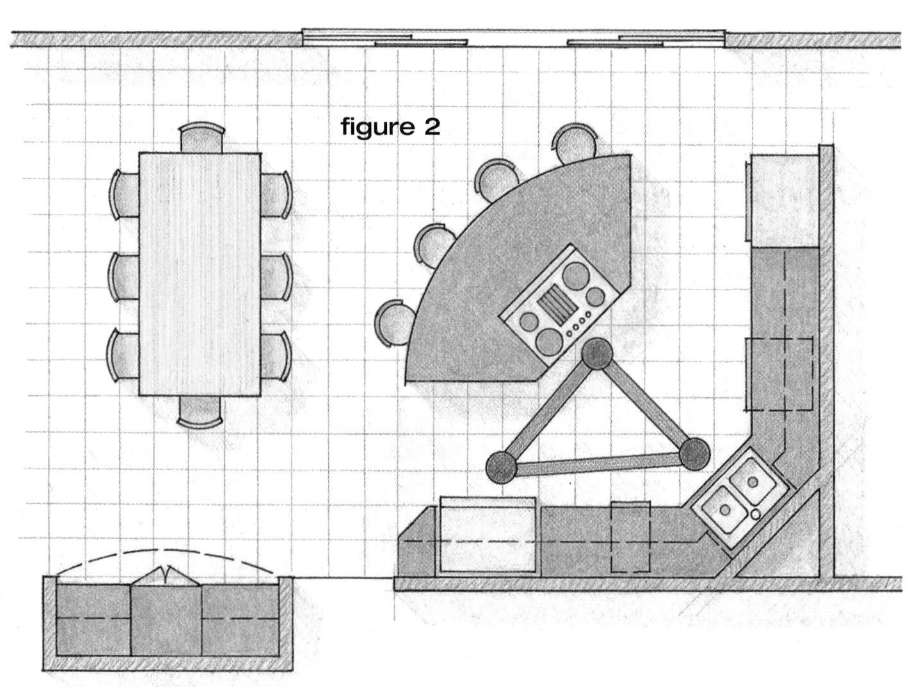

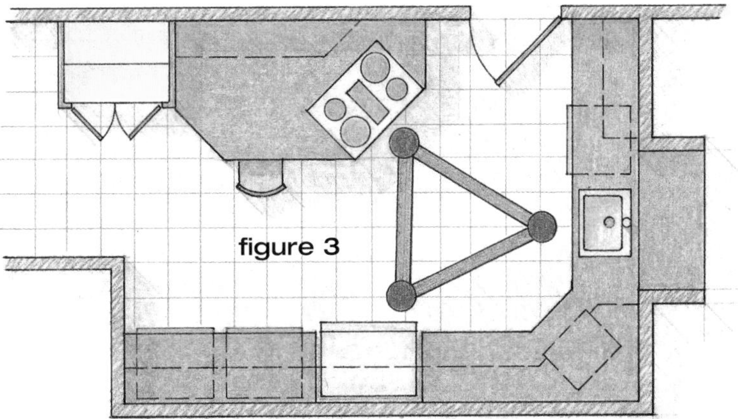

FIGURE 3
By placing the range at an angle across from the L, the oven door, when open, will not interfere with traffic from the entry into the kitchen.

ABOVE In this L-shaped plan, a serving bar forms a boundary between the dining room and kitchen.

RIGHT With the counters arranged along perpendicular walls, an L-shaped layout offers enough space for storage and displays.

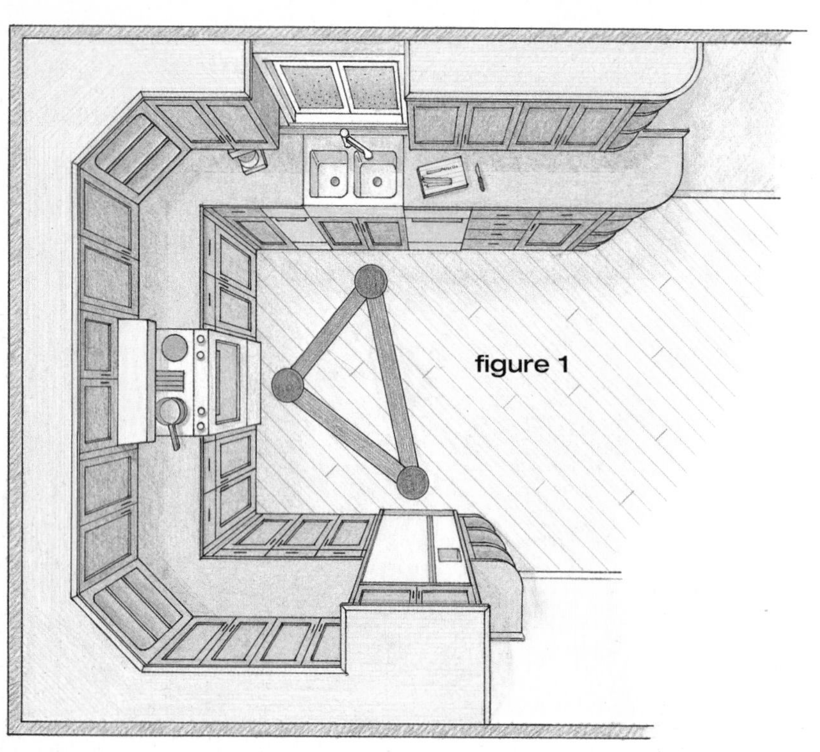

FIGURE 1 A typical U-shaped layout

BELOW AND OPPOSITE A hands-down favorite of design experts, a U-shaped kitchen boasts space for two cooks as well as multiple work triangles.

FIGURE 2 Large plans easily accommodate multiple work triangles.

FIGURE 3 This U-shaped layout creates an eat-in kitchen.

U-shaped designs are highly functional

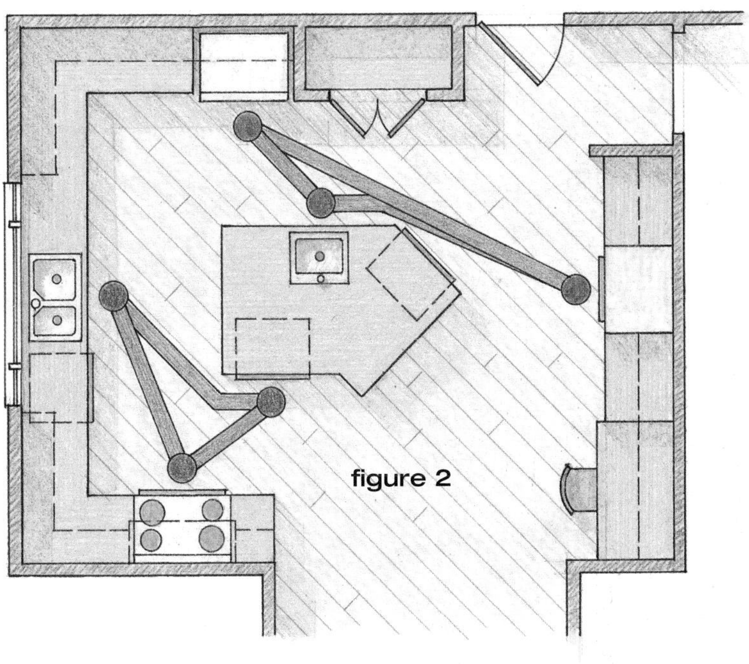

figure 2

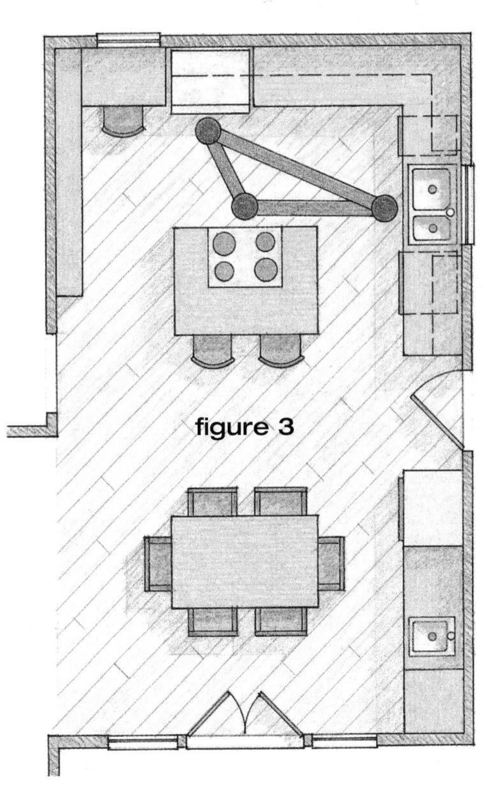

figure 3

a G shape adds a short “leg” to a U

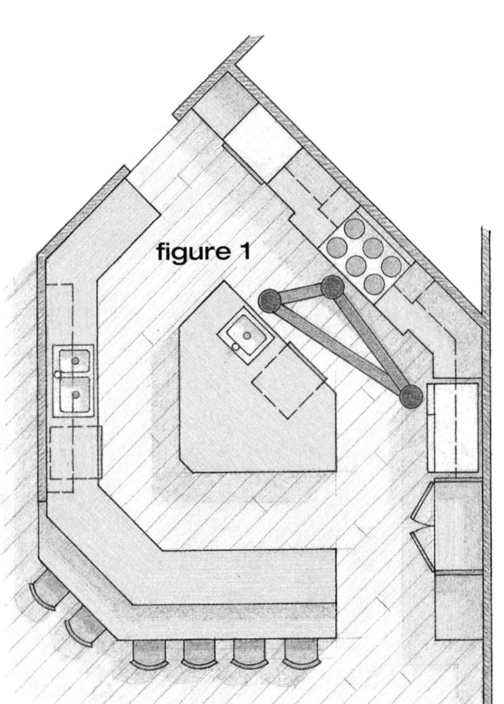

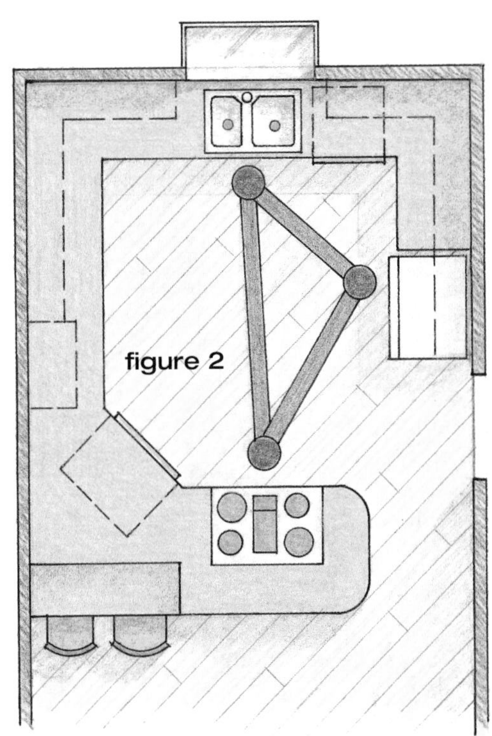

LEFT This configuration places the cooktop in the G created by the curved island.

FIGURE 1 A large G-shaped layout allows two cooks to work together and has a generous amount of work surfaces.

FIGURE 2 The typical G configuration is a U with the addition of a short leg—usually a peninsula.

RIGHT Enveloped by the G of the island, this compact kitchen ensures sociability.

islands and peninsulas

because no kitchen layout is absolutely perfect, consider beefing up yours with an island or peninsula. Islands improve function in several ways—they add counter space, hold a cooktop or sink, and provide storage or a surface for casual meals. Peninsulas perform similar functions and are often added to a U-shaped layout to produce a G. With cabinets accessible from both in and outside the work zone, peninsulas are a plus in busy kitchens.

RIGHT A transitional-style island provides a multipurpose expanse for prep, serving, and dining.

BELOW This large island holds many of the kitchen's appliances and also helps define the space.

define your work space

grace notes

Furniture-style legs keep this large, custom-built island from appearing bulky and awkward.

as well as your sense of style

islands help organize a large space into

distinct zones

OPPOSITE TOP This farmhouse-style kitchen appears old-fashioned, but the marble-top island holds many modern conveniences.

OPPOSITE BOTTOM This massive multipurpose island is loaded with storage and functions as the dominant design feature of this kitchen.

ABOVE Shaped like a pie wedge, this island creates separate work, dining, and storage zones.

roll with it

Do you yearn for an island that can move from one work station to another or roll into the dining room for serving? If so, look for one with casters on the legs. Thus equipped, the island will glide smoothly and then lock into place.

extend work surfaces and storage

TOP This contemporary island features multiple surface levels for storage, cooking, and dining.

LEFT A circular island helps soften the edginess of this striking Euro-style kitchen.

OPPOSITE The ornate carvings and classic hardware on this wooden island complement the Old World charm of the kitchen.

pot racks

Hanging in profusion over an island, copper cookware makes a gleaming design statement.

hearth & home

A stone fireplace in the kitchen provides a warm glow as well as a source of homebaked delights.

eat-in kitchens

Here's a scenario that's especially popular these days—you lovingly prepare food, enjoying the company of family and friends while doing it, and then sit down to eat, all in the same room. There are many ways to make this warm and friendly fantasy a reality, even in a small kitchen.

If your new or remodeled design will be large, you can simply place a dining table somewhere in the room, taking care to position it at least a few steps away from the food-preparation area. In a modest-sized room you might build in a banquette or a booth along one wall or in an alcove. Space-saving banquettes are actually benches—usually upholstered for comfort—that lie along one or two walls in a corner and face a table. Space for a booth can often be carved out of the kitchen floor plan, too, although most booths don't seat more than four people. Islands and peninsulas can also provide space for snacks or quick meals but wouldn't be comfortable for diners who want to linger.

OPPOSITE A black leather banquette enhances the luxurious feel of this Arts and Crafts-style kitchen.

RIGHT A glass-top table and curved banquette blend seamlessly into this contemporary kitchen.

BELOW Diners perched at this center island can take in the outdoor view from the large windows.

problem solver

A pullout table that is concealed behind a false drawer panel when it is not needed may be the answer when a full-size table is too large for a small kitchen.

three rules for the kitchen

- **Hide the mess** No matter how good the meal is, you don't want diners to have to look at the messy pots and pans that created it. If your dining table is near the work zone, shield cooking clutter with an island that's bar height—42 inches—on the table side and counter height—36 inches—on the kitchen side.

- **Keep the noise down** Eating in the kitchen is informal, yes, but don't let noisy appliances drown out all attempts at conversation. Dishwashers are the worst offenders. Invest in one of the super-quiet models, or make sure not to run the dishwasher at all until after dinner.

- **Lower the lights** Create a pleasant mood. "In my kitchen," says New York designer Rick Shaver, "the table is lit but I leave the undercabinet lights on in case I need something during the meal."

OPPOSITE The L-shaped island adds another work zone and a cozy banquette to this eat-in kitchen.

ABOVE Situated near windows that overlook a terrace, diners at this table can enjoy the light and view.

Go Green

Choose eco-friendly paints, stains, and wall-coverings. Look for "No VOCs" (Volatile Organic Compounds) on the label.

2

What's Your Style?

You've made an important decision—to remodel your kitchen and make it functional and inviting. But exactly what kind of look do you want? One that is traditional, country, or contemporary? The style that's right for you will probably harmonize with the design of your house inside and out. If the architecture is classical, a formal look may be right. Country styles seem to suit people who enjoy a casual and relaxed lifestyle. A contemporary design will be a good choice if you like clean lines and a minimum of accessorizing.

- **traditional**
- **country**
- **contemporary**

The owners of this contemporary kitchen chose black to complement an otherwise monochromatic palette of gray and silver.

traditional

When you have chosen the look you love for your kitchen, you will find that the cabinets set the stage. In traditional kitchens, where the ambiance is elegant, gracious, and just a little bit formal, cabinets are most commonly crafted of rich, gleaming woods, usually cherry or mahogany or any wood stained to resemble them. Ivory- or white-painted cabinets are another frequent choice, but the key to the cabinets is a rich, glossy finish and the look of fine furniture. For the cabinet door style, choose a raised-panel design and such architectural details as crown moldings and other millwork. Whether countertops are made of glossy, polished stone such as granite or marble, a solid-surfacing or plastic laminate look-alike, or one of the many strikingly beautiful and eco-friendly options such as concrete, recycled glass, or even paper, they may also feature rich details such as bullnose or beveled edges. Choosing countertop colors of deep green, dark gray, or black will add richness, as will wood floors or a classic black-and-white checkerboard pattern in ceramic or vinyl tile. One of the reasons for the popularity of this gracious style is its timelessness and the fact that it is unaffected by design trends that come and go.

OPPOSITE This traditional kitchen combines white-painted wood, light granite countertops, and classic subway tiles.

LEFT A warm beige paint on the walls marries well with the white window frames and creamy-hued countertops.

BELOW This kitchen uses color, including the robin's egg blue cabinets and sage and cream curtains to add country style.

coffee station

This little corner is reserved for an espresso machine. The granite countertop is stylish and practical as a heat-resistant surface.

clean, forever-classic

glass act

Frosted-, opaque-, textured-, wavy-, or etched-glass cabinet doors hide a multitude of sins. Behind them, cabinet contents look interesting but don't have to be neat as a pin. In addition, they don't show fingerprints as easily as clear-glass panels.

OPPOSITE Neat lines, granite countertops, and expanses of white cabinetry give this room its classic character. Glass cabinets display pretty serving pieces.

RIGHT In another classic-white kitchen, a tile backsplash and marble countertops reinforce the sleekness while adding texture.

TOP LEFT A three-arm chandelier finished with a mellow patina adds a touch of elegance and casts a warm and welcoming glow.

ABOVE The tile backsplash and oversized hardware suggest another time and place.

LEFT Old World style features painted finishes, ornate details, a stronger emphasis on stone, and cabinetry that resembles pieces of antique furniture.

the niche

A rectangle above the range consisting of tile set in a diamond pattern takes the place of a more ornate design yet manages to create a subtle focal point.

the elegance of Old World design

RIGHT This kitchen's most striking detail is the olive cabinetry, which picks up the green tones in the marble counters and contrasts beautifully with the dark brown islands.

BELOW In rustic and inviting kitchen, the tile backsplash leaves no doubt that there's an Italian chef at work.

OPPOSITE BOTTOM Wood ceiling beams, an enormous fireplace, and an arched doorway create the look of a traditional Tuscan kitchen.

tuscan tones

A "pop" of bright color, such as in this informal bouquet, enlivens the traditional Tuscan palette of olive, siena, and umber, which are the foundation for an authentic look.

a take on tuscany

timeless customs

What could be more continental than a frothy cappuccino? And what could be more appropriate in an Old World-inspired kitchen than a coffee station? The one pictured here has been created inside a bank of cabinets with slide-in doors. But aside from an espresso machine, what other elements go into creating what we call Old World style? The look is actually a mix of French and Italian with a little Greek and Roman classicism thrown into it, too. Nothing should look shiny or new. The overall effect is comfortable with obvious signs of wear and tear. Richness in color, material, and texture is also key—rugged limestone or tumbled marble; ceramic tile; mellow woods; and disparate elements that seem to have been lovingly added piece by piece over time.

Some kitchen designers and other experts in the field theorize that we love the country look because it recalls the warmth of Grandma's kitchen, conjures up romantic notions of the keeping rooms of old, or simply links us to what we believe was a simpler, gentler time. Whatever the reason, this is an extremely popular style, and opportunity for personal expression abounds. Informal and relaxed, country is a good choice for a casual lifestyle; and because the look of wear and tear is desirable, it suits busy families and active kitchens, too. Build your country kitchen around wood cabinets in a natural stain, a weathered or bleached finish, or a cheerful paint color. Neither elegance nor sleekness is the goal; so mismatched cabinets, freestanding unfitted pieces, or open shelves filled with dishes are also appropriate. Wood floors are ideal but homey patterns in vinyl or tile would also work. Almost anything goes for countertops, but especially something that's earthy —a rustic stone or tile, for example.

country

There are many offshoots of this basic look—English country, cottage, Victorian, and Arts and Crafts, to name a few. If you're the country-kitchen type, one of these variations is sure to please you. Shown here is another variation on the theme, the new look of American country, a slightly more sophisticated style with sleeker lines and fewer accessories than its predecessor.

RIGHT This design takes country to a sophisticated new level. White bead-board and homespun hardware intermingle with antique piano stools and elegant granite counters for an uptown approach to down-home charm.

OPPOSITE TOP The kitchen is open to an inviting family dining area composed of an antique pine bench, table, and grandfather clock.

OPPOSITE BOTTOM An antique stove, retrofitted for modern family meals, adds instant nostalgia and authenticity to this kitchen.

show it off

Glass-front cabinets are both functional and attractive, and the look can open up your space dramatically.

country style has looks

creating cottage style

An amalgam of English country and Victorian bungalow, the cottage kitchen ranges from rustic to refined. An all-white scheme puts the room shown here in the refined category, but all the key elements of the overall style are represented—painted, furniture-style cabinetry, plate racks, and glass knobs. Other versions of a cottage kitchen might include colorful, mismatched, and slightly worn-looking cabinets and vintage furniture and accessories.

color bites

In a kitchen with a mostly neutral color scheme, a small pop of color is all that's needed to add pizzazz.

OPPOSITE TOP This kitchen is a great choice for those who love to commune with nature. The warm tones of the wood cabinets make it cozy, and the many windows frames a woodsy view. The enormous stone fireplace in the great room completes the rustic ambiance.

OPPOSITE BOTTOM LEFT This urban apartment has a farmhouse feel thanks to the right combination of accessories and wood finishes.

OPPOSITE BOTTOM RIGHT In addition to providing an ample work surface and extra storage, this sturdy island makes an important decorative statement. Unglazed ceramic tile is a natural choice underfoot.

that range from rustic cabin to cozy cottage

american farmhouse versus

a lived-in look

OPPOSITE TOP AND BOTTOM Simple cabinets, a period-style sink, a collection of milk pitchers, and an antique grocery scale contribute to this farmhouse kitchen's ambiance.

BELOW Glass front cabinets, matte finish floor tile, and plate racks for displaying collectibles give this kitchen an English country air.

English country style does not derive from the great estates of the English provinces but from modest homes and bungalows that retain the pleasant clutter of many generations. To re-create this style, choose cabinets with a patina of age and details such as plate racks, niches, and glass fronts. For floors, wood or matte-finish tile works well; countertops may be stone, solid-surfacing, or wood—any material that does not look shiny and new. The desired effect resembles an Old World kitchen, but the colors are lighter, and personal collections of English china are key.

english country

LEFT In this distinctive ranch-style kitchen, rough-hewn woods and expanses of unpolished stone combine with rich metals and glass to create an envelope of casual luxury.

INSET A tree trunk serves as a table base, flanked by chairs constructed of reclaimed timber.

BELOW Half-timber ceiling beams and log paneling on the walls give the kitchen a hand-built look.

southwestern accents

Go Green

To connect with nature's cycles, reserve fruit and vegetable scraps for recycling into compost to feed your garden.

LEFT Diagonal-pane windows frame a cheerful mosaic wall design in this straight-from-Provence-style kitchen.

BELOW The mélange of elements contributing to this French style look include white-painted cabinetry, colorful tiles, ladderback chairs, pottery, and copper accents.

French-provincial ingredients

The contemporary style had its origins at the end of the nineteenth century when artists, architects, and designers rebelled against the fussy and cluttered design sensibility that prevailed throughout most of the Victorian era. Their rebellion manifested in simplicity and the use of natural materials. As the look evolved it continued to emphasize natural materials but became more and more streamlined. For a time, in the 1970s and '80s, when newly emerging technology was impacting the culture, a "high-tech" look was de rigueur in many kitchens. These designs were sleek and hard-edged; articulated in the neutral tones of stainless steel, stone, and glass; kitchens looked almost like laboratories. Although contemporary style remains pared-down for the most part, it has warmed up considerably since then.

contemporary

The backbone of today's contemporary kitchen is frameless, flat-panel cabinetry with clean lines and simple hardware. Wood finishes, particularly maple, cherry, and birch in lighter tones, are common choices. Cabinet doors made of glass and metal—often aluminum—are popular because they go well with sleek contemporary appliances. Natural surfacing materials—especially stone, tile, and concrete—or solid-surfacing and laminate versions dominate surfaces. The Retro Modern, or Midcentury Modern, look that can be seen in home furnishings is also influencing kitchen design. Sleek and industrial in a 1950s-70s way, it may not be for everyone, but it has a growing following.

Go Green

Many of today's eco-friendly paints and finishes work just as well as traditional formulas.

OPPOSITE True to the contemporary philosophy, these Euro-style cabinets are without embellishment, except for the oversized brushed-steel hardware. Industrial-style stainless-steel countertops are chic and easy to clean.

ABOVE This updated contemporary kitchen is streamlined but far from sterile. The black wood cabinets lend drama, while the open shelving of the island displays glassware and bottled water like modern works of art.

RIGHT Black wooden chairs in the dining area add another layer of warm sophistication and complete the monochromatic scheme.

retro modern

ABOVE The chartreuse and gold mosaic tile behind the cooktop is echoed in the island.

LEFT Red suede and chrome bar stools are reminiscent of a 1950s cocktail lounge.

RIGHT Touches such as the stools and pendant lamps qualify this kitchen as retro-chic.

revisiting the recent past

A decorating style that revisits midtwentieth-century designs, Retro Modern is a manifestation of the contemporary genre. The retro chic philosophy does not suggest that you entirely recreate the look of the era; you can incorporate just a few telling details. For example, to retro-fit your kitchen with a '50s flavor, you might add diner details, such as chrome stools topped with red-leather seats or plastic-laminate countertops with the reissued boomerang pattern. Retro-style appliances are available from several manufacturers, too.

today's contemporary kitchens use natural materials

pull-out pantry

You can squeeze ample storage out of a narrow space with vertical shelving installed on a rolling track.

If you are fond of contemporary interiors but afraid that a kitchen designed in this clean-lined, unembellished style is doomed to look cold and clinical, think again. The contemporary kitchen has evolved over the last few decades, and the "high-tech" laboratory look is out, replaced by a warmer, friendlier version. Today's contemporary-style kitchens are still simple, spare, and equipped with the latest technology, but a new focus on wood for the cabinets and the restrained use of color as an accessory makes them as appealing and inviting as any traditional or country-style kitchen. Study the rooms on these two pages to see the influence of wood and other softening elements in state-of-the-art yet personal spaces.

LEFT The attractive vertical grain that runs through these bamboo cabinets provides a pleasing textural counterpoint to the stainless-steel hardware, range hood, and appliances.

ABOVE This rollout pantry is just one of the many ingenious options available for making food, prep, tableware, and cleanup storage space efficient and convenient.

eclectic style

An eclectic kitchen is very personal. It brings together elements from different styles and eras and makes them visually cohesive. It's not easy to pull off, but this advice from designer Rick Shaver of Shaver-Melahn in New York City should help. "There must be a common thread, be it color, texture, architectural detail, even collectibles," says Shaver, who designs furniture as well as interiors. The kitchen shown here relies on architectural detail to unite its disparate elements. Another eclectic design might be held together thematically by displays of collections such as bowls, kitchen utensils, or transferware.

OPPOSITE TOP The mix of patterns, colors, and materials in this contemporary kitchen make it one-of-a-kind.

OPPOSITE BOTTOM The pleasingly mismatched dining set lends casual charm to this small kitchen.

RIGHT There's a little bit of everything in this city kitchen, from a classical column pedestal to funky wood dining stools.

create your own a style mix

3

Choosing the Cabinets

Cabinets are often called the backbone of the kitchen not only for their impact on the design, but also on your construction budget. The cabinets you choose will establish your basic layout and organize all of the accoutrements of food preparation. Appliances, countertops, and wall and floor finishes flesh out the basic structure established by the cabinets. Get your money's worth by shopping and buying smart. In this chapter you'll find information to help you make the best choice for your needs.

- **design impact**
- **styles and options**
- **price points**
- **smart storage**
- **measuring for cabinets**

Your choice of cabinets is an important one. They should be functional and sturdy, and they should define your sense of style.

LEFT This cleverly designed unit has multiple purposes: it houses the refrigerator, as well as storage and display spaces, and serves as a floating wall between the kitchen and family room.

ABOVE Fine-furniture detailing enhances the simple elegance of these glass china cabinets.

BELOW Anything but shy and reserved, these richly stained oak cabinets set the stage for a one-of-a-kind kitchen design.

wow factor

Unexpected touches, such as these multitoned wood cabinets, lend heightened visual drama to the kitchen.

Cabinets perform two important functions in the kitchen—they store and organize the necessities for cooking, and they determine the design of the room. Other factors, such as countertop and flooring materials, appliances, wall and window treatments, and accessories, contribute to appearance. But cabinets are the most visible element and are therefore most responsible for the overall look.

In the kitchens of the last century, furniture was used haphazardly to hold dishes, pots and pans, and utensils, but they didn't necessarily match each other or anything else in the room. That mismatched, "unfitted" sort of look is popular again today with some homeowners, but most people prefer cabinets cut from the same design cloth to provide a unified look for the kitchen.

design impact

Once you have chosen the layout that meets your needs and the design style that reflects your taste and personality, you're ready to go cabinet shopping. Take your time. Whatever style you have settled on will be available from every major manufacturer of kitchen cabinets. Visit showrooms, look at calalogs, log on to company Web sites, and study the choices within the category you prefer. Get cost estimates, too. Armed with cost information and a rough idea of how many cabinets you'll need, you'll have a ballpark budget for the cabinet portion of your new kitchen, which according to experts, is about 40 percent of the total.

A foolproof way to figure how many storage cabinets you'll need is to empty the contents of your present ones and combine everything you want to store. Each pile of dishes, pots and pans, flatware, table linens, and cookbooks will represent one, or maybe more, of the cupboards and drawers you now require. If this method proves too disruptive and time-consuming, study your present storage situation and estimate how much more you will need, allowing for items that you'll accumulate over time.

TOP RIGHT The appeal of this otherwise simple cabinet design is enhanced by an unexpected color choice.

BOTTOM RIGHT These contemporary cabinets offer good looks, high quality, and careful construction.

LEFT A creamy finish and leaded-glass panels contribute to the appeal of these English-style cabinets.

BOTTOM LEFT Looking for glamour in the kitchen? Choose rich-looking cabinets with ornate trim.

RIGHT Stately cabinets with recessed panels and a pale olive finish make a strong design statement in this gourmet kitchen.

details that deliver

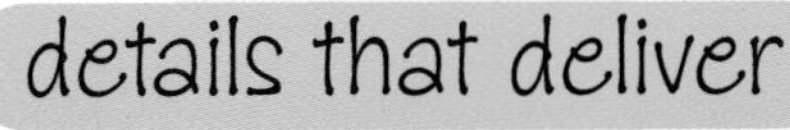

Want to heighten visual drama in your kitchen? Finishing the fridge to match the cabinetry creates a seamless look that is unbroken by appliances.

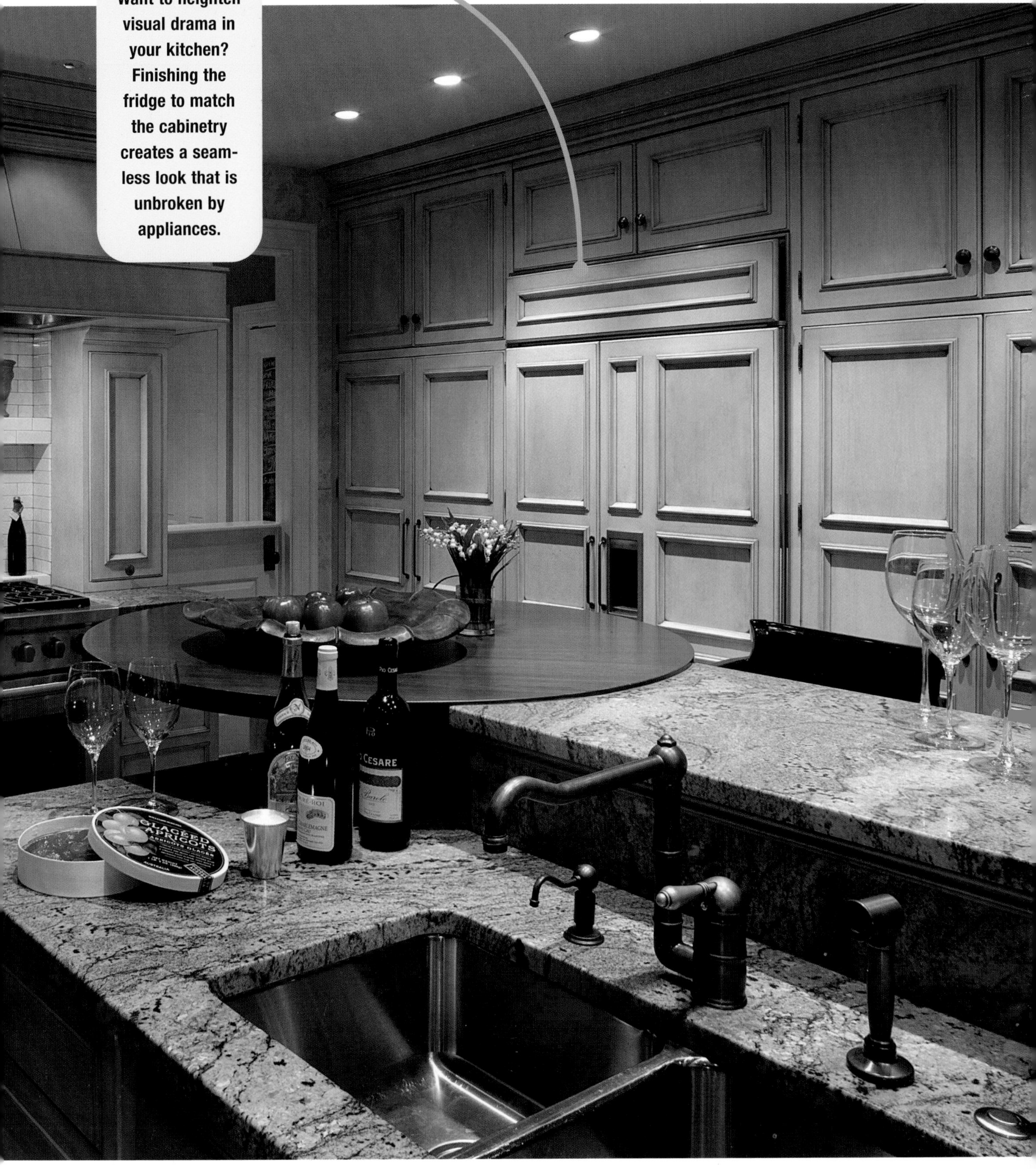

FAR LEFT These white cabinets provide a crisp contrast to the sunset-hued walls.

LEFT Furniture-like details make this range hood look especially elegant.

BELOW The mellow finish of the cabinetry provides the backdrop for this eye-catching tile backsplash.

frame a cooking area with cabinetry

Custom-designed cooking zones are distinguished by range-hood enclosures that match surrounding cabinets, blend seamlessly with the overall design, and create appealing focal points.

styles and options

thousands of manufacturers produce attractive cabinets in a huge variety of styles, finishes, and prices. But not all of them are well built. Before you buy cabinets, scrutinize their construction details. Beware of drawers that are nailed, glued, or just stapled together. Well-made drawers should support about 75 pounds when open. Cabinet cases should measure at least ½ inch thick all around, and interiors, including rear surfaces, should be finished. Adjustable shelves are another sign of quality. Make sure they measure at least ⅝ inch thick to prevent bowing. Look for solid hinges that don't squeak and that allow doors to open fully.

Some fine cabinets are made of solid wood, but a plywood box with solid-wood doors and frames also offers good structural support. Less pricey but acceptable units mix plywood supports with medium-density fiberboard doors and drawer fronts, or feature a laminate finish over high-quality, thick particleboard. However, stay away from drawers made of thin particleboard, as they won't be sturdy enough for daily use.

cabinet door style choices

Door styles are strictly decorative. Styles pictured, left to right: reveal-overlay panel; frame and panel; flat panel; beaded frame and panel; square raised panel; curved raised panel; bead-board panel; and cathedral panel

OPPOSITE LEFT Stacks of cheerfully mismatched china are on full display in this glass cabinet.

OPPOSITE RIGHT A contemporary-style refrigerated drawer holds enough beverages for a party.

LEFT The design of these glass-panel cabinets frames and enhances the beautiful collection.

ABOVE Refrigerated drawers place often-used foods in close proximity to work counters. Another convenience—the interior lights up when you open the drawer.

Treated with a light honey hue to contrast with the dark wood ceiling and the black cabinetry of the island, the dramatic vent hood and cupboards filled with collectibles command attention.

framed versus frameless construction

In framed construction, a rectangular frame outlines the cabinet box to add strength and provide a place to attach the door. The doors on frameless cabinets are laid flush over the box. No frame is visible, and hinges are often invisible as well.

Frameless A European concept that took hold here in the 1960s, frameless cabinets are a standby in contemporary kitchens. The doors fit over the entire cabinet box for a sleek and streamlined look.

Framed Cabinets with a visible frame offer richness of detail that is appropriate for traditional and country kitchens and their many design cousins.

LEFT Just enough space was carved out for this recessed cabinet, which is deep enough to handily tuck spices next to the cooktop.

RIGHT Glass-front cabinets in this butler's pantry display fine china and serving pieces.

BELOW This center island's storage options include large bins for holding bulk items, such as pasta and grains.

options

As you shop for cabinets, think about building specialized areas where family and friends can come together—a home office, a place for kids to do crafts or homework, a bar, a baking zone, even an entertainment center. Inquire about cabinet options that incorporate convenient features.

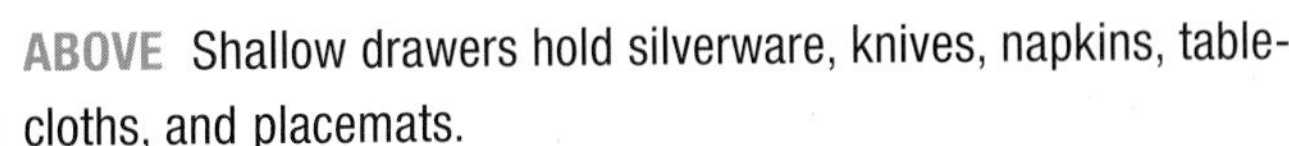

ABOVE Shallow drawers hold silverware, knives, napkins, tablecloths, and placemats.

BELOW The deep drawers under this cooktop are roomy enough for very large pots and pans.

OPPOSITE TOP LEFT Shelves glide out when you need to retrieve something; when closed, the clutter disappears.

OPPOSITE TOP RIGHT An efficiently organized drawer keeps coffee, tea, and spice canisters within easy reach.

OPPOSITE BOTTOM LEFT An old-fashioned skirt covers a smoothly gliding undersink drawer.

OPPOSITE BOTTOM RIGHT With their hint of rustic appeal, these wooden shelves lend a farmhouse touch to this kitchen.

get a handle on it

Cabinet hardware is such an important element these days that some designers call it "the jewelry of the kitchen." As the four examples below illustrate, you can find hardware to suit any style of kitchen, from ornate to graceful to old-fashioned to streamlined.

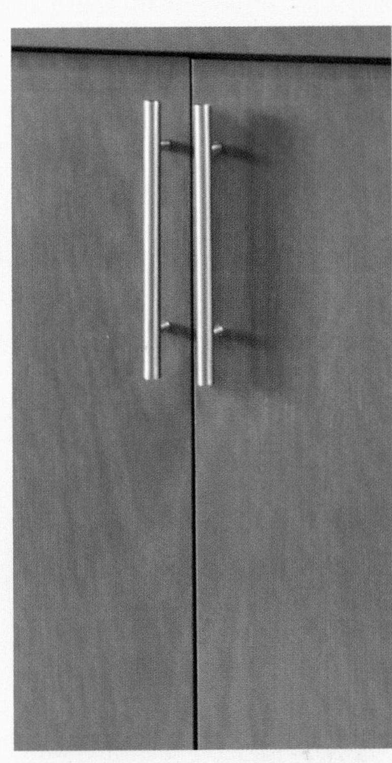

Go Green

When selecting cleaning products for your kitchen, look for ones that use plant-based ingredients, not petroleum-based ones. Petroleum is a nonrenewable resource that is energy intensive and causes pollution during extraction and refining.

price points

there are several ways to buy cabinets for your new kitchen. **Knock-down (KD)** units go home with you the same day, and if you can install them without hiring a professional, the price is right for a tight budget. Mass-produced **stock** cabinets, issued only in standard sizes and in limited styles and finishes, are also an economical choice if quality is good. **Semicustom** cabinets are restricted to standard sizes too, but the variety of styles, finishes, interior options, and accessories is much greater, expanding design options considerably. **Custom** cabinets, available through better cabinet manufacturers, architects, designers, or cabinetmakers, are built to your exact specifications and measurements. You'll pay a premium price, but you'll get a one-of-a kind kitchen with a personalized look and endless storage possibilities.

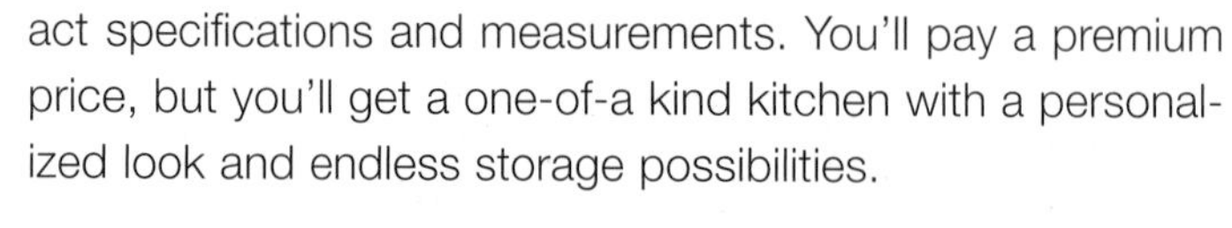

ABOVE LEFT The cheerful yellow finish on this storage trolley proves that today's modern kitchens are anything but sterile.

ABOVE In this country kitchen, dark bead-board cabinets contrast warmly with a hammered-tin backsplash.

LEFT Solid construction and sturdy hardware are evident details in this simple cabinet design.

OPPOSITE Getting the right height and function are important design factors; these translucent cabinet doors fold down for convenient access in the prep area.

Take advantage of the many storage options available to help your kitchen hold a lot more. Begin by taking upper cabinets all the way to the ceiling to hold items that are used infrequently. Outfit lower cabinets with helpful extras such as rollout shelves, lazy Susans, tray dividers, and tilt-out bins. Chrome-plated backsplash systems can be fitted with cookbook holders, spice racks, and wire baskets. Use pullout wicker baskets to make the best use of space in deep drawers.

smart storage

look high and low for places to beef up storage

ABOVE RIGHT Twin pantries flanking the refrigerator keep food items handy.

RIGHT Smart design makes the most of available space.

OPPOSITE Tableware and collectibles are displayed in classic English style.

taking stock

Manufactured cabinets available in standard sizes can be a very affordable and even high-quality option. Most experienced kitchen designers can help you create a custom look using stock cabinetry.

LEFT A large carousel keeps condiments, sauces, and packaged items within easy reach; pullout shelves hold everything from wine to linens.

OPPOSITE TOP You'll never lose the cinnamon if it's stored near the cooktop.

storage savvy

Standard cabinets are not the most efficient places to store pots, pans, and their elusive lids. Special tall pullout cabinets do the job, too. Deep drawers are also great—the pots lift out easily; and as the drawer slides out, you can see its entire contents.

OPPOSITE LEFT Pantry basics are cleverly concealed behind an antique gate set on a sliding track.

OPPOSITE RIGHT Another option for storing spices is a specially designed drawer.

clutter free is the key

TOP LEFT Sliding baskets hold seasonal produce.

TOP RIGHT Roomy divided drawers tame kitchen odds and ends.

LEFT A concealed cupboard is built from normally unused space.

CENTER RIGHT Large shelves display oversize pots and pans.

BOTTOM RIGHT Recycling bins are neatly hidden.

ABOVE A fully outfitted baking center increases efficiency.

LEFT Loads of storage is tucked behind these sleek cabinets.

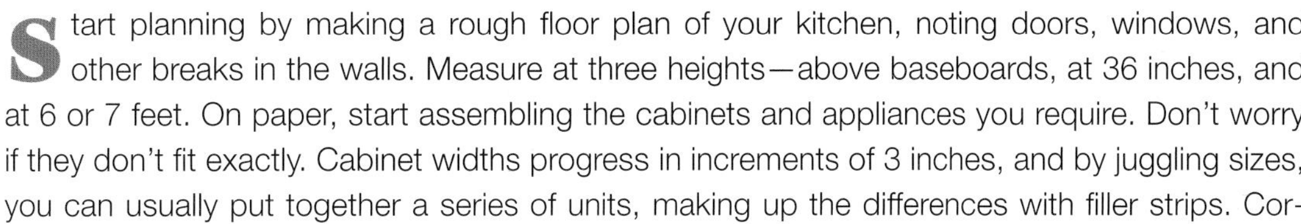

Start planning by making a rough floor plan of your kitchen, noting doors, windows, and other breaks in the walls. Measure at three heights—above baseboards, at 36 inches, and at 6 or 7 feet. On paper, start assembling the cabinets and appliances you require. Don't worry if they don't fit exactly. Cabinet widths progress in increments of 3 inches, and by juggling sizes, you can usually put together a series of units, making up the differences with filler strips. Corners can be tricky. Ask your designer or contractor about specialty units, such as blind bases or corner bases. Or consider adding a corner sink or a peninsula to make use of corner space.

measuring for cabinets

typical dimensions

Alter these typical dimensions to suit your needs. For example, many people prefer a 37½-in. counter height, and tall people are more comfortable working at an even higher counter.

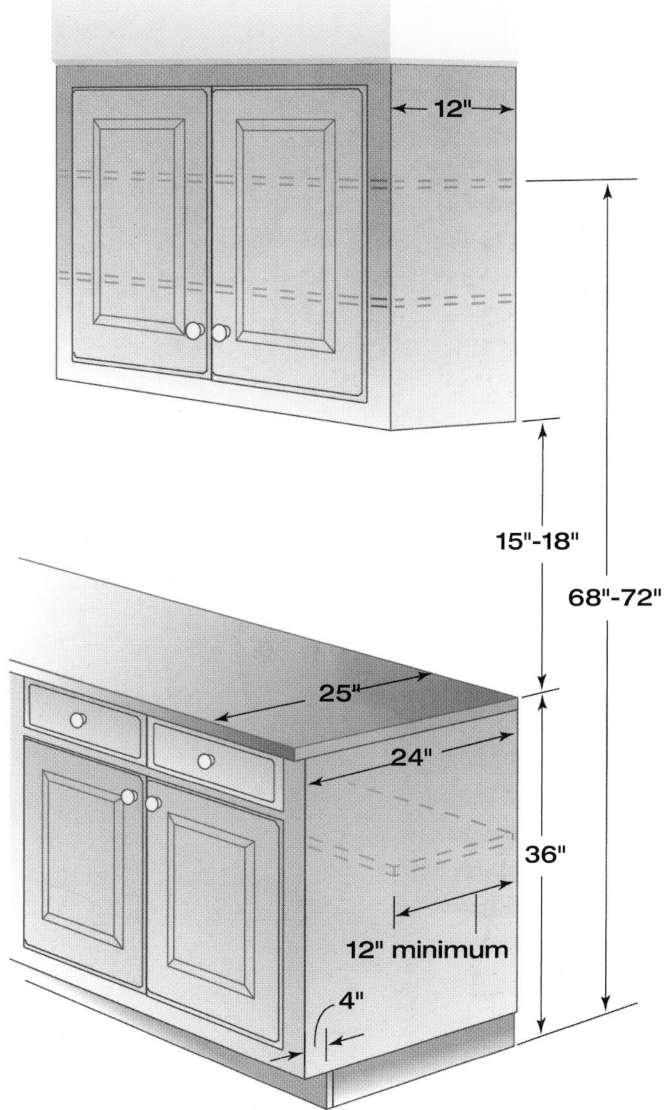

These custom cabinets were carefully crafted to fit the curved walls of this kitchen.

glass dilemma

Clear-glass cabinet doors require more neatness than many people can manage. Instead, try tinted glass, which has equal appeal but camouflages contents.

the shape of things

STANDARD CABINET DIMENSIONS (in inches; ranges in 3-in. increments)

Cabinet	Width	Height	Depth
Base unit	9–48	34½	24
Drawer base	15–21	34½	24
Sink base	30, 36, 48	34½	24
Blind corner base	24 (not usable)	34½	24
Corner base	36–48	34½	24
Corner carousel	33, 36, 39 (diameter)	X	X
Drop-in range base	30, 36	12–15	24
Wall unit	9–48	12–18, 24, 30	12, 13
Tall cabinet (oven, pantry, broom)	18–36	84, 90, 96	12–24

take advantage of nooks and crannies

OPPOSITE Custom-made cabinetry strikes the right note in the kitchen of a late-nineteenth-century house.

RIGHT Small but important storage areas can put wasted space to work. These niches keep a collection of oversized bowls on display.

the right height

According to kitchen planners and designers, the most accessible storage compartments are positioned roughly between eye level and knee height. Organize your storage so that often-used items fall into this range; then stash items that you rarely use above and below these points.

4

On the Surface

Although cabinets will be the most recognizable element in your kitchen, the surfaces—walls, floor, and ceiling—that surround them will also affect the look of the room. Selecting materials and finishes wisely can make the difference between a visual hodgepodge and a harmonious design. But it's not all about looks. There are practical considerations, too. If the surfaces you select are easy to maintain and able to withstand daily wear, you'll spend less time cleaning and more time enjoying your new kitchen.

- **wall treatments**
- **flooring**
- **ceilings**

A cool blue-gray on the cabinets complements the gleaming tile and stainless-steel accessories in this striking kitchen.

While you're focused on cabinets, appliances, and countertops for your new kitchen, don't let the walls get lost in the shuffle. The way you finish the walls will define your style and pull the design together.

Paint is the easiest and most economical wall treatment, unless you choose a decorative finish that requires a specialist. And if you want to trim the budget a little, you can do the painting yourself. Whatever color paint you decide to use, select a washable finish. And remember—ceilings don't have to be white. Painting them a lighter version of the wall color or a very pale blue is more interesting.

Wallcoverings, such as a washable vinyl, cost a little more than paint but are still quite economical to apply, especially if you do it yourself with prepasted and pretrimmed rolls: a variety of colors, patterns, and coordinating borders are available, with new ones introduced yearly.

wall treatments

Paneling, another smart surfacing choice, is the most effective way to cover up imperfections in an existing wall. The word "paneling" refers to planks or sheets used as a wall surface, and it doesn't have to look like the imitation "wood-grain" panels you may remember from "finished" basements of the past. In fact, some paneling is quite elegant and expensive. There is a middle ground, however, with a variety of woods or wood look-alikes that can add warmth and character to your kitchen. Wainscoting, which is paneling that goes to chair-rail height, is a popular choice for country-style kitchens.

OPPOSITE TOP Matte-finish tiles in gray and buff form geometric patterns reminiscent of a quilt in this country kitchen.

TOP LEFT Stacked-stone walls resemble a fireplace hearth and enrich other warm tones in the kitchen.

OPPOSITE BOTTOM The bold colors in this mosaic-tile backsplash transform the kitchen from ordinary to warm and vibrant.

LEFT Light pine log walls and a paneled ceiling give this kitchen the snug feeling of a country cabin.

decorative paint finishes

Many professional paint techniques for creating unique wall finishes are surprisingly easy to master. Most of these decorative styles employ the same formula of a base color that shows through the broken color and translucence of one or more top coats of colored glaze. The differences lie in whether the glaze is added or subtracted on the surface and how it is moved about. Stunning results can be achieved by using a crumpled rag, but can be even more striking when applied with a special brush or tool. Always start with a well-prepared surface and a good base coat of solid color.

Sponging

Ragging

Stippling

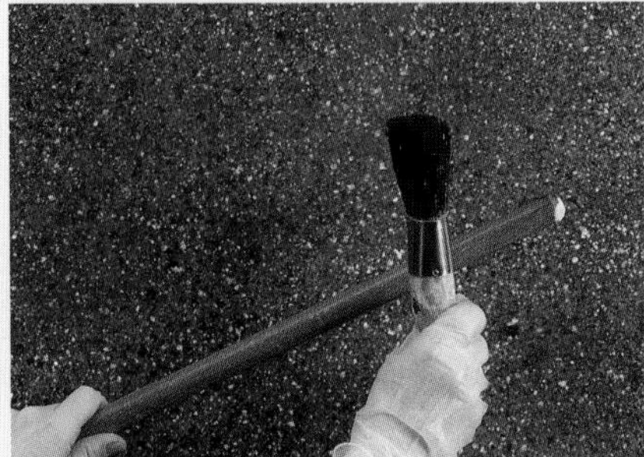
Splattering

Combing

- **Sponging** is perhaps the easiest of all the techniques, as the goal is a random, uneven pattern. Sponging creates an illusion of depth by having multiple layers of broken color over a base color. Simply load the sponge with glaze and dab. Don't over-sponge or you'll get muddled and splotchy areas instead of the fields of dotted color you are after. Use the sponging technique for walls, ceilings, flat-surfaced furniture, and cabinets. For subtle depth, use varying shades of one color over the base.

- **Ragging** is good for walls, doors, and flat-surfaced furniture. The success of this finish depends on the colors in your glaze, the contrast to the base coat, and what type of material is used to add or subtract one or more coats of glaze. For an elegant and mellow effect, use soft, clean, lint-free cotton squares.

- **Stippling** works well for any surface, including curved molding. With this method, the glaze is moved and transformed with a finely bristled stippling brush. Stippling makes a delicate, slightly elevated, consistent finish. The technique demands a smooth, well-prepared surface. Both the base coat and the glaze should be oil-based.

- **Splattering** This method showers the base coat with tiny droplets of paint or glaze. One way to deliver the paint is to load an oval sash brush and then tap the ferrule of the brush against a stick or another brush handle. The technique can create a deep, textured surface that is alive with color. Try to load the brush with the same amount of paint each time. This will help you achieve an even distribution of color.

- **Combing** creates visually interesting patterns such as stripes and distinct lines. By using different tools, some which you can make yourself, patterns are created where the glaze is lifted off. As with all of decorative paint techniques, move your hand steadily to a stopping point. If you muddle an area or stop midpoint, the surface must be reglazed and started over. Colors can be vivid to highlight the patterned effect or more subtle for a slight suggestion of pattern.

Distressed, glazed finishes in a variety of soft colors help make the soaring dimensions of this Southwest kitchen feel cozier and more inviting.

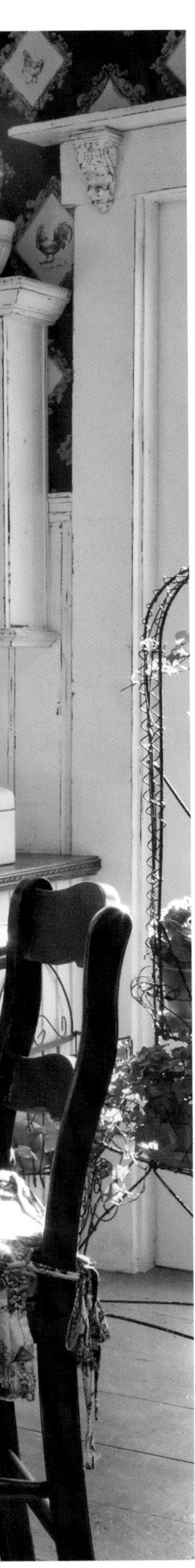

LEFT Mixing several patterns and distressed-wood finishes adds personality to this cottage-style kitchen.

ABOVE Simple white cabinetry looks fresh and bright when combined with tomato red walls and accents of yellow and soft green.

wallpaper and paint

When it comes to kitchen wall treatments, there is only one hard-and-fast rule—use washable paints and cleanable, nonporous wallcoverings. Here are a few other decorating tips for using color and pattern:

- Bold, deep paint colors will warm up the kitchen; cool colors create calm; prints and patterns add liveliness and cheer.
- Not sure that a particular color or pattern will work? Apply paint or a large wallcovering swatch to a piece of poster board; hang it on the wall; and see how you like it as the day changes. Still love it? Live with it for a week before making a decision.
- To establish harmony throughout your house, choose a wall treatment that's in sync with the rooms that adjoin the kitchen.

popular trimwork profiles

Greek and Roman details are a part of so many decorating styles that it's hard to find ornamental trim without some kind of classical design. The ogee shape, for instance, appears on everything from interior trimwork to exterior cornices to table edges. Here are some of the basic molding shapes and motifs that have withstood the test of time.

Torus/Astragal

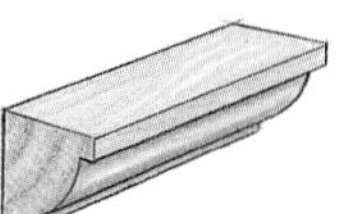
Ovolo

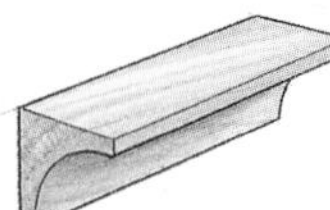
Cavetto

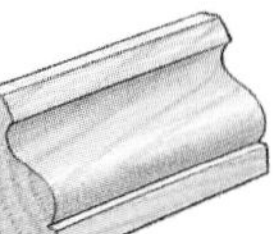
Band Molding

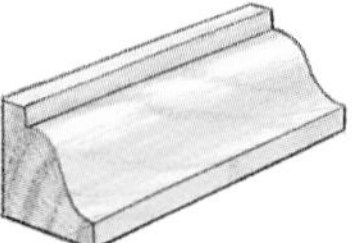
Ogee

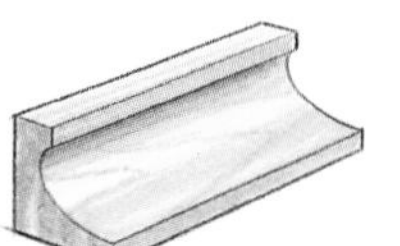
Scotia

Wall Molding

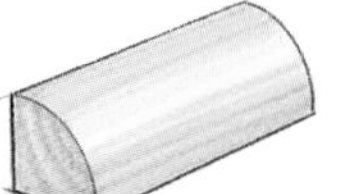
Quarter-Round

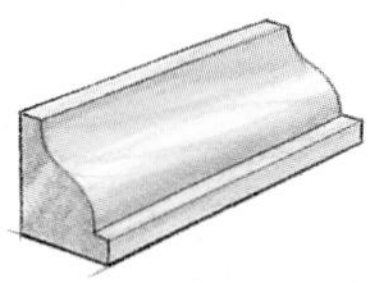
Reverse Ogee

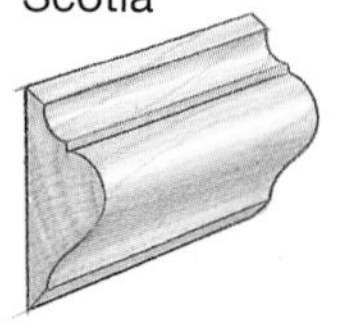
Panel Molding

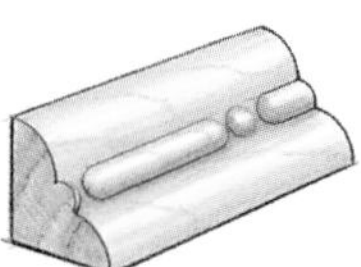
Bead-and-Reel

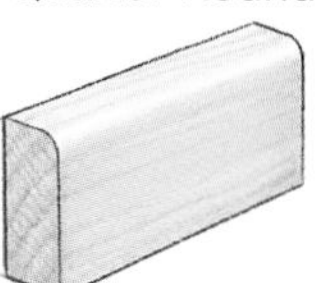
Bullnose

trimwork

Architectural trim—a category that includes door and window casings, moldings, baseboards, and columns—is the crowning glory of a well-planned room, like a ribbon that puts the final beautifying touches on a gift package. It's important that you choose ornamentation that matches the style and proportions of your kitchen and the architecture of your house. Choices vary from simple to elaborate, as the drawings below illustrate. Ornate detailing works well in traditional rooms; simpler trim is more suitable for casual or contemporary settings. If you're after a really fancy effect, you may have to enlist a cabinetmaker, but check your lumberyard or home center for precut or ready-made possibilities.

Fret

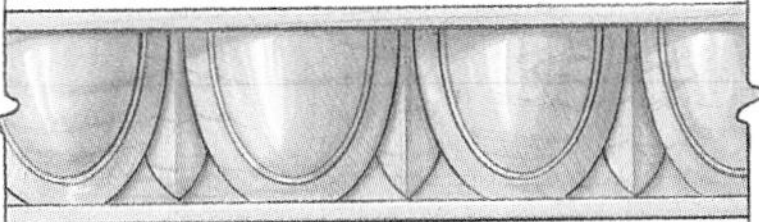

Egg-and-Dart

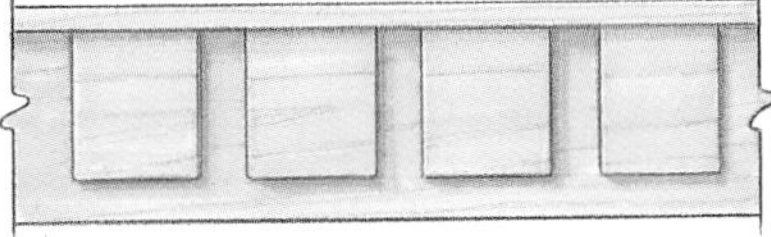

Dentil

OPPOSITE The white ceiling and window trim add crispness to these sunny yellow walls.

ABOVE White stands out against tomato red walls in this sophisticated kitchen.

RIGHT A mosaic tile border lends additional distinction to this rich wood paneling.

classic columns

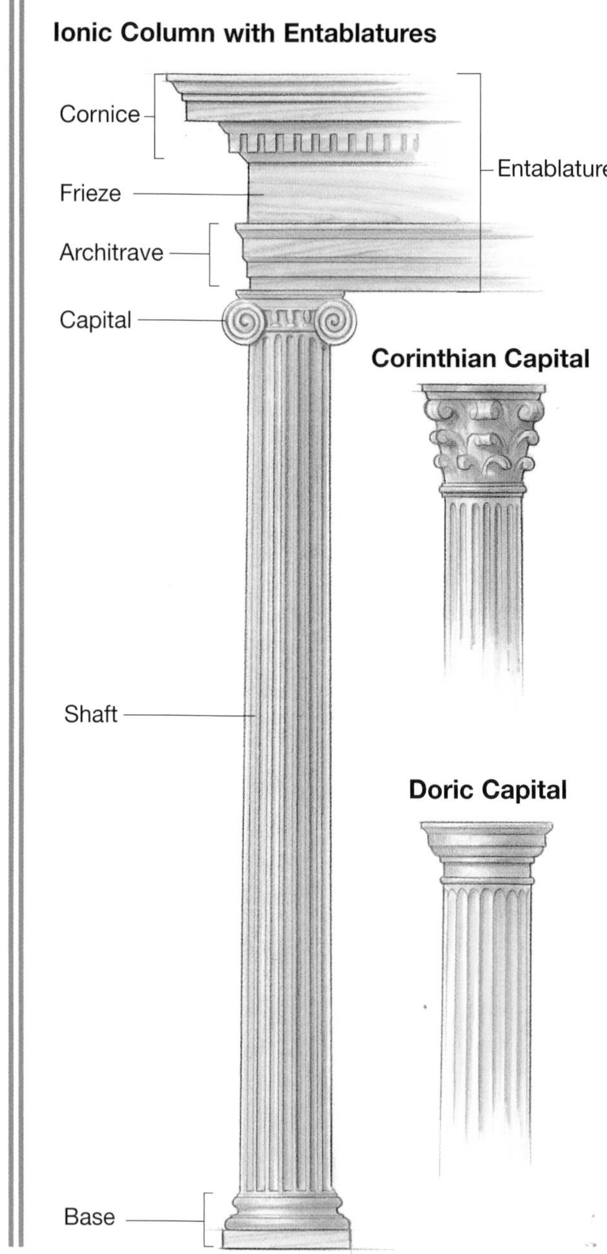

TOP Classic wooden columns create a visual separation between this kitchen and dining area.

LEFT Stately white columns match the cabinetry and draw attention to the high ceilings.

Pilaster Construction

Capital

Collar

Shaft

Plinth

Base

RIGHT A row of single columns and an elaborate coffered ceiling lend weight and importance to the design of this kitchen and adjacent dining area.

door and window casings

Victorian-Style Mitered Casing

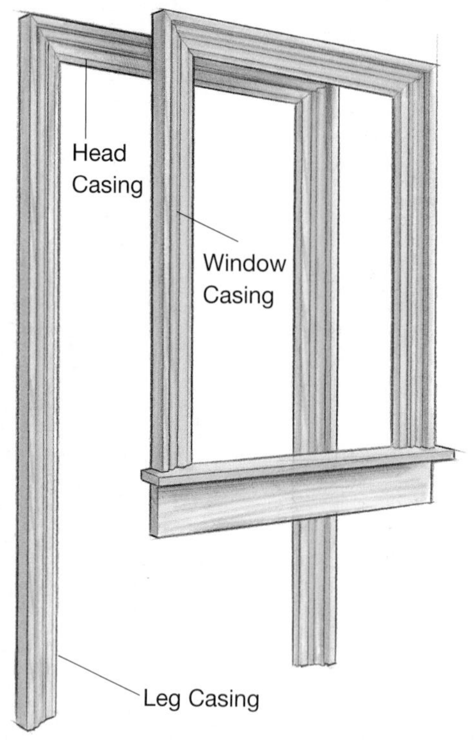

Bellyband Casing with Rosette

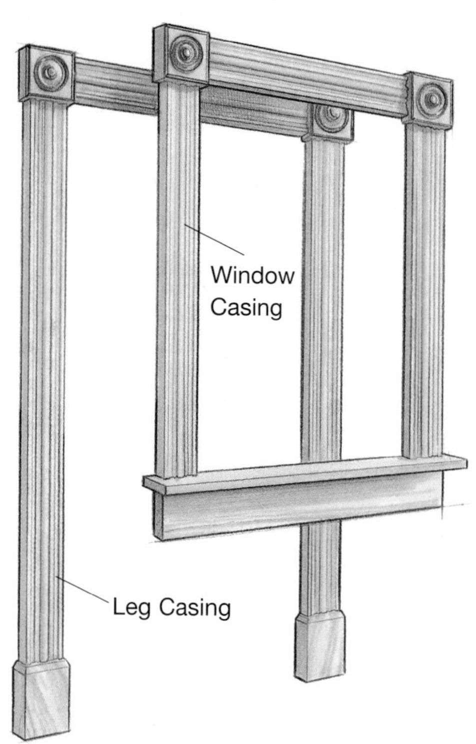

Arts and Crafts–Style Casing

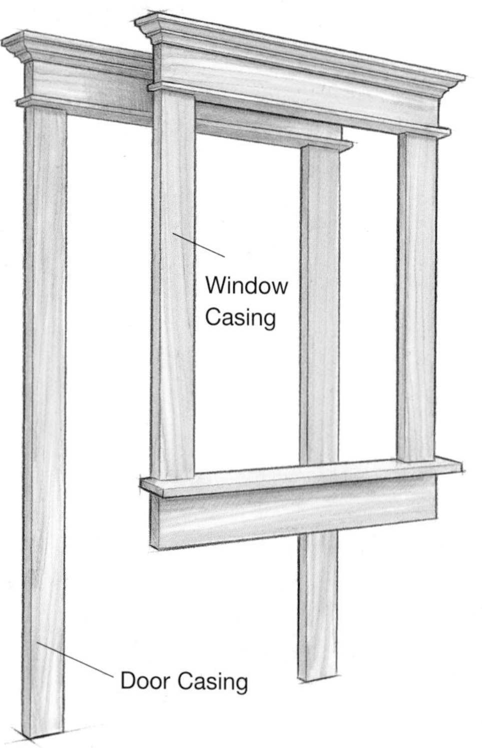

Fluted Casings with Decorative Head

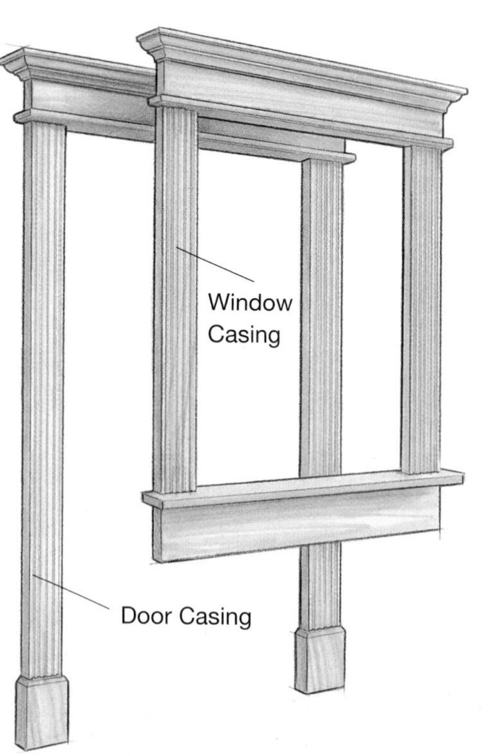

ABOVE Simple framing around this window draws the eye to the outside.

OPPOSITE TOP Wood casings are the focal point of these contemporary windows.

OPPOSITE BOTTOM Arts and Crafts-style grillwork accentuates these large windows.

Go Green

Recycling can pay handsome dividends, such as these antique bricks salvaged from old buildings.

flooring

Most of the flooring materials on the market today combine good looks with low maintenance and durability, all of which are important qualities for use in the kitchen. Because looks are important in this highly visible room, you'll want a floor that blends with the cabinets and other elements that you have chosen. When you go shopping, keep design harmony and appropriateness in mind. Wood works well with virtually any kitchen style, but stone, suitable for a contemporary room, may not be right for some traditional kitchens, and a minimalist material, such as concrete, must be used judiciously. Also, ask questions about the cleanability of the materials you like. No flooring is completely maintenance free, of course, but some require less attention than others. How much cleaning are you willing to do? The answer to this question will help you choose. Here's another important question: how much comfort do you want underfoot? Some materials—wood, vinyl, and laminate, for instance—"give" better than others. If you'll be on your feet for long periods of time preparing complicated recipes for large numbers of people, you may want to go for a material's cushioning effect and forgo something less forgiving, such as ceramic tile and stone. Learn about degrees of durability, too. Most modern materials are designed to stand up well to wear and tear, but if your kitchen is an especially high-traffic area, with kids and pets running through it, you'll need something that's especially tough. Select the highest quality and most durable product that you can afford, and avoid "bargain" materials that you will have to replace in a few years.

ABOVE A ceramic-tile floor in a checkerboard pattern lends a country-style touch to this contemporary kitchen.

OPPOSITE TOP LEFT Reclaimed brick pavers bring a rustic, antique character to this kitchen.

OPPOSITE TOP RIGHT A wide-plank wood floor is a natural choice for a simple kitchen design.

OPPOSITE BOTTOM The brilliant natural color variations in this slate-tile floor are complemented by the cherry cabinetry.

accent mark

The bold checkerboard pattern on this kitchen floor was achieved by alternating a light and dark stain on the wood.

the warmth of wood

Wood floors introduce warmth and a feeling of comfort to the kitchen, but some types work better than others in this busy room. Oak, maple, ash, and other hardwoods stand up better than softer pine, fir, or cherry to the pounding a kitchen floor takes. A wood floor finished on-site with oil or wax has a beautiful sheen, but it will need yearly refinishing. A polyurethane finish lasts longer and requires no stripping, waxing, or buffing. High-quality prefinished flooring, an increasingly popular alternative, eliminates the time, mess, and toxic fumes of the floor-finishing process. There is also increasing interest in hand-scraped wood, which is hand distressed for a rustic appearance. It looks old, but its finish is up-to-date and durable. Properly finished wood floors are easy to maintain, and minor spills are not a problem. However, continued exposure to water, around the sink or dishwasher for example, could cause warping or buckling.

OPPOSITE TOP LEFT Deeply stained and highly polished, this floor adds warmth to the kitchen.

OPPOSITE TOP RIGHT The focal point of this salvaged pine floor is its pronounced grain.

OPPOSITE BOTTOM The weathered look of this floor complements the antique farm table.

LEFT This oversized harlequin pattern makes a pleasing, easy-care design statement.

BELOW The medium stain on this oak floor stands up to all kinds of dirt and moisture.

ceramic tile and stone

Ceramic tile and stone are popular kitchen flooring materials, and no wonder. Ceramic tile is durable, moisture proof, easy to maintain, and available in such an enormous range of colors, sizes, and shapes that its design potential is practically infinite. Tiles that mimic stone are particularly popular right now. So are the stone materials themselves, especially granite, slate, limestone, and soapstone, all of which also offer durability and easy maintenance, but they must be sealed. Ceramic-tile costs range from moderate to pricey; stone is generally more expensive. If you choose any of these materials, put safety first and select textured, matte finishes that provide slip resistance. The down side? Ceramic tiles and some types of stone can crack if something heavy falls on them—whatever falls will likely break, too. Other possible drawbacks: these materials are noisy when you walk on them; and they are cold and hard underfoot. What's new and trendy? Tinted, painted, and stained concrete.

LEFT This multicolored slate floor coexists harmoniously with the seagreen cabinetry.

ABOVE Classic white marble tile adds a formal note to this contemporary kitchen.

OPPOSITE TOP Slate tiles in hues of gray, taupe, and beige pair well with almost any design.

OPPOSITE BOTTOM New fabrication techniques have made stone a more affordable option for many homeowners.

smart investment

Stone not only increases the value of your home, it enhances the pleasure of living there.

RIGHT Natural stone offers a wide palette of colors and textures, no two of them ever identical.

BELOW Silver-gray ceramic tiles complement the brushed metallic surfaces in this contemporary kitchen.

OPPOSITE This tumbled marble tile floor unites the dining and cooking areas in this galley-style kitchen.

natural stone is like artwork in your kitchen

basic tile shapes and patterns

The basic floor tile measures 12 x 12 in. with ⅛- to ¼ -in. grout joints.

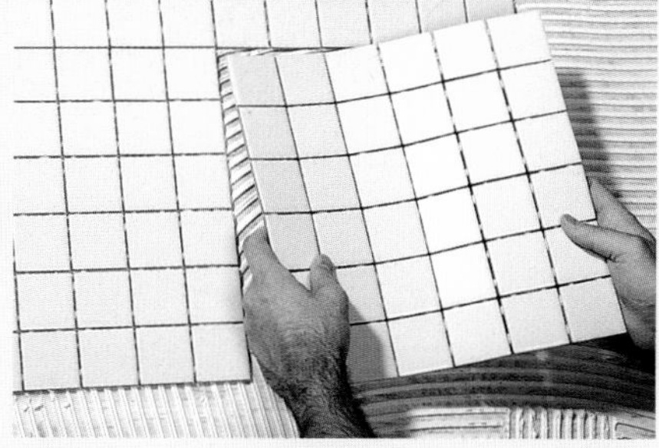

Sheet-mounted tile will look like individual mosaic tiles when installed.

Rectangular tiles can create basketweave patterns.

Combining different shapes allows you to create a variety of patterns.

Hexagon-shaped tiles create an interlocked pattern.

Multicolor and **multisize tiles** are available in sheets.

vinyl and linoleum

Resilient vinyl flooring has been hugely popular since the 1960s. Low-cost, low-maintenance, and durable, it is available in a multitude of colors and looks. In addition, it has a certain amount of built-in cushioning, making it comfortable while you stand and work. It's smart to invest in a high-quality product with a tough wear layer and a generous amount of cushioning. Every vinyl floor will show wear eventually, but a medium-toned background with a definite pattern will look good longer than a light or white background with very little pattern. Vinyl comes in sheets or tiles.

Linoleum, which lost favor because it required waxing and sealing, is now available presealed, so it's easy to maintain. It is pricier than vinyl, but durable, comfortable underfoot, and available in a modest array of colors and patterns in sheets or tiles.

OPPOSITE Resilient flooring in a contemporary style enhances this sleek kitchen.

TOP LEFT This resilient-vinyl sheet flooring resembles flagstone tiles.

BOTTOM LEFT This attractive vinyl floor is also comfortable underfoot and easy to clean.

RIGHT Oversized resilient-vinyl floor tiles look clean and modern.

BELOW Scored and speckled sheet vinyl provides the look of stone at a fraction of the cost.

BE HAPPY

laminate provides advantages over the real thing

Go Green

Not only do today's laminates help preserve forests, but they don't harbor allergens in the home.

laminate and engineered wood

Laminate flooring can look like stone, tile, or other materials, but it is best known for its realistic mimicry of wood strips or planks. The visible layer of this multilayer product is a photographic image, which is then covered with a tough melamine coating. Bonded together under high pressure, the layers add up to an extremely durable floor that under normal circumstances can handle heavy kitchen traffic and withstand such mishaps as scratches, burns, and stains. Walking or standing on a laminate floor is comfortable, and it's easy to maintain and economical, although somewhat more expensive than vinyl. Most laminate floors "float," which means they are not nailed or glued to an underlayment, and they can be installed over most other materials, including wood, concrete, vinyl flooring, or ceramic tiles. There are a number of laminate-flooring brands, and quality varies. To get the best product for your needs, ask about thickness, durability, and the life expectancy of the flooring. Because a damaged laminate floor cannot be recoated or repaired, it's important to look into warranties as well.

Engineered wood, like laminate, consists of several layers—typically three to seven—that are bonded together under heat and pressure. The top layer, a hardwood veneer, is available in almost any wood species. As a result of the layered construction, manufacturers claim that engineered wood is less susceptible than solid wood to damage from moisture or changes in humidity. More expensive than laminate, but less than solid-wood products, engineered wood can be installed over a variety of subfloors.

OPPOSITE TOP This faux-walnut laminate floor is gorgeous and stands up to foot traffic.

OPPOSITE BOTTOM Wood laminate in a cherry finish adds warmth without breaking the budget.

LEFT Pecan look-alike flooring works well in this contemporary kitchen.

ceilings

The ceiling? Just paint it white—nobody notices it. If that is your attitude, you're missing a wonderful opportunity to introduce detail and warmth to your kitchen—and to inexpensively eliminate existing flaws while you're at it.

Even a simple coat of paint on the ceiling can make a difference. A light, neutral, or pastel shade of paint will be more interesting than white and will increase the feeling of light and spaciousness in the room. A medium or dark hue will create coziness and intimacy.

Ceiling tiles and panels take things a bit farther by adding texture of various kinds and becoming part of the room's design. There are many types available—some with a subtle textured look; others with more definite, decorative patterns. Metal tiles that re-create the appearance of pressed-tin ceilings common in turn-of-the-last-century rooms are also available in a variety of sizes, patterns, and finishes, including tin, copper, and brass. They are sure to make a big impact when added to a country or period-style kitchen. Your lumberyard stocks sections of tongue-and-groove and bead-board planks that resemble porch ceilings of the past, another way to bring the charm of the past to a kitchen of the present. Before you embark on a ceiling treatment, be sure that it's in keeping with the feel of your house in general and with the style of your kitchen in particular.

OPPOSITE This classic tin ceiling provides subtle architectual interest thanks to its creamy satin finish.

RIGHT Wood beams, newly installed to create rustic charm, look like they've always been there.

BELOW The look of an antique pressed-copper ceiling tops off this traditional kitchen.

5

Major Appliances

The kitchen is the heart of the home, and appliances are the heart of the kitchen. But hold on to your hat—these days there are enough choices to make you dizzy. The first thing you'll notice is a new look. Many appliances are so sophisticated and beautifully designed that they almost qualify as furniture. Another trend—convenience. You can customize equipment to suit your cooking style, mix and match fuels, order features that think for you, and save energy. Before you shop, assess your budget and your needs.

- cooking
- ventilation
- refrigeration
- dishwashers
- laundry

There's a lot to love about this professional-style kitchen fitted with high-end appliances and gleaming finishes.

cooking

Although most families are busier than ever, they still love home cooking. And the manufacturers of today's cooking appliances are making it easy to prepare fresh meals in short order. Some new ranges and ovens roast or bake foods in a fraction of conventional cooking times. And a suit-yourself approach allows you to customize these appliances according to your cooking style, using either gas or electric, or a combination of the two. The influence of professional equipment, still going strong after more than a decade, can be seen in both the look of conventional ranges, ovens, and cooktops, and their performance, particularly the ability to control heat precisely. For example, commercial-style hi-lo burners can stir-fry at a searing 15,000 Btu or melt chocolate at a simmering 500 Btu. (Btu stands for British thermal unit, the measurement for heat output.) A dual-fuel range combines gas burners with an electric oven, and a separate cooktop can feature both gas and electric cooking elements. For two-cook kitchens, minicooking stations, called "hubs," can be configured as you wish, with one or two burners plus a steamer, a grill, or a deep fryer, for example. Warming drawers are hot again, a convenience for families on different schedules and for entertaining. In the midst of this speed and convenience, quality is paramount. Buy the best you can afford, even if you have to sacrifice special features.

OPPOSITE Well equipped for serious cooking, this kitchen includes a range, two wall ovens, and a powerful range hood.

RIGHT A commercial-style range has what a gourmet cook wants—three ovens, multiple burners, grill, griddle, and a huge exhaust hood.

BOTTOM RIGHT A restored 1930s stove appeals to nostalgia lovers.

ranges

Ranges come in several styles. With unfinished sides, **slide-in** (below) and **drop-in** (bottom) ranges are least costly. Slide-in models fit between two cabinets; drop-in models are installed on a base matching the cabinets. **Freestanding ranges** have finished sides and can stand alone.

lighten the load

This six-burner, continuous grate design lets you move heavy pots by sliding rather than lifting them.

types of cooktops

Gas cooktops, above left, start up fast, cook evenly, and are easy to control. Coil-style **electric cooktops** heat up quickly but cool slowly; they cost less than gas cooktops but can be more costly to operate. Also electric, ceramic-glass resistance and halogen cooktops, above right, heat up very fast; their sleek glass surface is easy to clean. **Induction** types have glass surfaces and cook by heating the cookware, not the cooktop. Like gas, induction cooktops offer quick response and precise control, but cost more and require cookware that contains iron.

OPPOSITE This pro-style gas cooktop boasts three continuous cast-iron grates, which create a larger cooking surface, and six burners, which offer precise heat control that ranges from simmer to searing.

RIGHT Four heating elements with nine zones offer optimal heat control in this electric cooktop. A bridge zone connects two elements to provide a larger cooking area.

customizing a cooktop

These days, selecting cooking options is as creative an endeavor as cooking itself. The concept of hubs, fresh from Europe, has made possible minicooking centers that may contain a gas burner and an electric element, plus a grill, griddle, or any combination of them. Larger cooktops can also receive this individualized treatment. The result—you can put together a cooktop that precisely suits your needs and install a second separate cooking station for another cook or smaller meals.

OPPOSITE This five-burner professional-style gas cooktop fits easily onto a modest-size work surface.

RIGHT This gas rangetop can be customized with an infrared griddle or charbroiler.

BELOW The unusual burner style on this gas cooktop places the controls in the center.

hot stuff

Features once considered premium, including smoothtops, self-cleaning ovens, and stainless-steel finishes, are now standard on many ranges.

ABOVE A streamlined microwave and under-the-counter oven help to unclutter the work aisle.

RIGHT This 60-in. dual-fuel range has a gas cooktop and two electric, convection-system ovens.

OPPOSITE TOP This injectable steam-powered oven prepares foods quickly and healthfully.

OPPOSITE BOTTOM Step-saving stacked ovens allow you to defrost food in the microwave, then roast it in the oven.

ovens

Conventional gas and electric ovens cook via heated air; pricier electric convection models add one or more fans for faster, more even cooking and browning. Steam ovens cook food quickly and, some say, more healthfully. Microwaves, the least costly option, cook very fast but don't brown foods. In a big hurry? The new speed ovens, which combine convection and microwave technologies, reportedly cook eight times faster than other methods. Even faster—and more expensive—are ovens that mainly use light (high-intensity halogen bulbs) to cook foods. They'll roast or bake foods in a quarter of the time required by conventional ovens. But unless the recipe you are preparing has been programmed into the oven's computer chip, you'll have to experiment at first to get the cooking time right.

sizing ventilation fans

No matter how attractive the hood may be, it is the fan in the system that actually takes the air out of the kitchen. Fans are sized by the amount of air they can move in cubic feet per minute (CFM). Here are some guidelines to help you size the ventilation fan to suit your needs: multiply the recommended CFM at right by the linear feet of cooking surface. Note: the length of the ductwork, the number of turns in the duct, and the location of the fan's motor also contribute to the size of the fan needed.

- Ranges and cooktops **installed against a wall:**
  Light Cooking: 40 CFM
  Medium to Heavy Cooking: 100 to 150 CFM

- Ranges and cooktops **installed in islands and peninsulas:**
  Light Cooking: 50 CFM
  Medium to Heavy Cooking: 150 to 300 CFM

ventilation

Ventilation systems are perhaps not as sexy as top-of-the line cooking equipment, but without one your kitchen will smell like a down-at-the-heels diner in no time. A hooded ventilation system, installed directly over the cooking surface, is the most effective way to expel smoke, grease, and nasty odors. The hood captures cooking air as it rises, and a fan expels it outside through a duct. Place your range hood so that it overlaps the cooking surface by 3 inches on each side and sits from 24 to 30 inches above it.

Hoodless downdraft ventilation, used with island cooktops, forces the air above the burners through a filter, then out of the house via ductwork. It's not as effective as a hooded system but better than a ductless fan, which can't do a good job.

OPPOSITE The marble backsplash and counters combined with a customized range hood give this cooking center a one-of-a-kind look.

ABOVE Restaurant ranges require large hoods and powerful ventilating systems.

LEFT A burnished copper exhaust hood coordinates with the walls and cabinets, adding plenty of pizzazz to the cooking area.

the range hood's role in the new home hearth

OPPOSITE TOP Here, a custom hood with wood trim hides a powerful exhaust system. The metal hood section boasts a custom-finished patina.

TOP LEFT This example of a redesigned "hearth" includes a mantel-style range-hood cover fitted with a clock. Both incorporate fine architectural details.

LEFT European-inspired hearth-like cooking centers have become increasingly popular, as this custom design (and the two above) illustrates.

ABOVE A sleek chimney-style hood can be used with a cooktop or a range.

cooling

refrigerators and freezers have come a long way. Current models have sleek good looks and smart features we could barely have imagined a decade ago. And all of them consume less energy. The most important advance, however, is the ability to customize these appliances and their features to suit your cooking, cooling, and entertaining needs.

As always, you have a choice between a separate refrigerator and freezer and the more common combination of the two within one model. Combination models include refrigerator-and-freezer side-by-side, freezer-on-top, or freezer-on-bottom configurations. Side-by-sides keep both fresh and frozen foods easily accessible, but only the largest sizes can efficiently store the bulkiest items. With bottom-mounts, fresh foods are at eye level, but freezer access requires bending; top-mounts do the reverse, so your choice may depend on which section you need to access most. Nowadays you can rethink this large, central cooling appliance in favor of modular or smaller under-counter refrigerators or freezers placed at various zones in the kitchen according to need.

There's big news inside the new cooling equipment, too. Storage is more flexible and customizable. There is room in some models for platters of party food, two-liter soda or wine bottles, bulky frozen foods, and other items you used to have to jam in to fit. "Elevator" shelves slide up smoothly, and glide-out shelves make it easy to find items that can get hidden in the back. Some models have two thermostats or dual compressors so that humidity levels in fresh-food and freezer compartments can be controlled separately; that way, lettuce won't wilt in order to keep ice cream frozen, for example. Another plus—there is no transfer of odors from one compartment to another. Inside the fresh-foods compartment, there may be several temperature zones so that you can store fruits and vegetables differently from meats, dairy products, or beverages. Express features on some refrigerators chill certain foods superfast or cut thawing time in half. Cooling equipment is now designer equipment too, especially at the high end. Some stainless-steel units have the commercial look that many people love; retro, 1950s-style units with up-to-date interiors come in bright colors that really stand out. If you're not going to call attention to your chic refrigerator you can follow another significant trend by integrating it with the look of your kitchen. Select a built-in or 24-inch-deep unit that fits flush with the cabinets or hides behind cabinet doors.

OPPOSITE These drawers look like part of the cabinetry, but they open to reveal two small refrigerators convenient to the prep area.

TOP LEFT A handy pullout shelf allows for easy unloading of groceries directly into the fridge.

ABOVE To reduce the bulky look of a refrigerator adjacent to a full-size freezer, the homeowners covered both with elegant wood paneling.

LEFT A wine cooler built into the island is easily accessible during parties yet out of the cook's way.

classy cover-ups for

custom refrigeraton

In the old days, the refrigerator ruled. We put the bulky combination unit in a central place, if possible, then clustered our work zones around it to save steps. These days, thanks to the flexibility of modular cooling units that can be placed anywhere in the kitchen, we are no longer slaves to that one immovable behemoth, which is a special blessing for multiple-cook kitchens. We can provide point-of-use convenience in the bar area with a compact under-counter unit and an ice maker, or supply a secondary cooking station with a drawer-style refrigerator or freezer. Many combinations are possible—so get creative and customize.

OPPOSITE Looking like a handsome piece of furniture, this customized built-in design is clad in wood overlays that match the cabinets.

LEFT In a traditional-style kitchen, overlay panels make the built-in wine cooler look like one of the cabinets.

TOP RIGHT Under-counter cooling is an especially hot kitchen trend, with modules designed for specific functions and point-of-use convenience.

BELOW Create a built-in look for under-counter appliances using custom-made panels that blend with the cabinetry.

RIGHT See-through glass doors, an idea borrowed from the pros, are handy if you're willing to keep refrigerator contents neat and tidy.

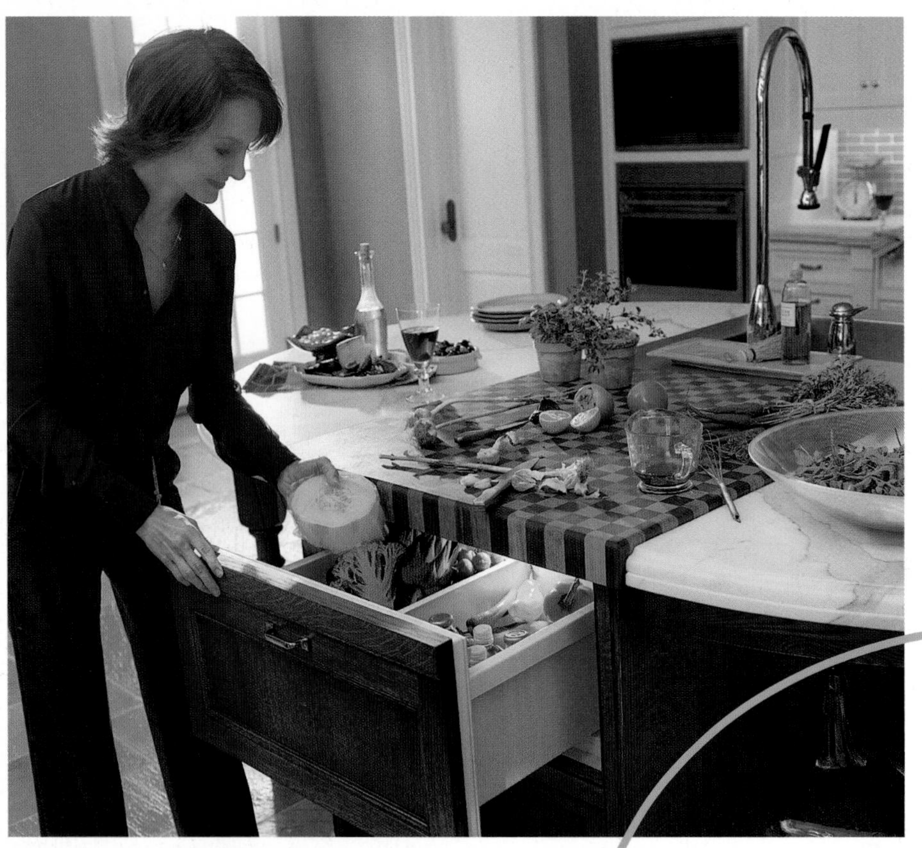

LEFT This secondary food-preparation area is equipped with a refrigerator drawer for storing produce.

BELOW A refrigerator, freezer drawers, and wine cooler are combined in this brushed stainless-steel model.

OPPOSITE Don't let the retro styling fool you—this wine cooler is state-of-the-art.

Go Green

Replacing an older fridge with a new Energy Star-qualified model saves enough energy to light the average household for nearly four months.

today's dishwashers are whisper

LEFT This dishwasher's height makes loading and unloading more comfortable for everyone.

OPPOSITE TOP Thanks to dual drawers, you'll never have to unload the dishwasher if you don't want to.

OPPOSITE BOTTOM For consistently small loads, a compact dishwasher may be sufficient.

dishwashers

Using a dishwasher will save you about four hours of labor a week, according to the Association of Home Appliance Manufacturers. As you shop for this important labor-saving device, you'll find some significant improvements in energy efficiency and noise levels. Some new models use fewer than 5 gallons of water for a standard cycle; others heat the water faster. In some of the fancier units, sensors detect the amount of soil on the dishes and automatically select the proper temperature and number of cycles. With this feature, you'll no longer need to run the appliance on an energy-wasting maximum setting for every use.

Dishwashers are also reportedly 50 percent quieter these days, provided you choose a well-insulated model. For a simpler noise-control option, select a delay-start feature and run the machine after you've gone to bed. Energy costs may be lower then, too. Dishwashers measure 18 or 24 inches wide. Large families or those that frequently entertain will need the bigger model and maybe a second one. For consistently small loads, an 18-inch unit or a compact dishwasher drawer may be sufficient. Consider these other features and options: stemware racks; split baskets for small loads; zone cleaning; strong, normal, and soft water jets; extra-large capacities; and dual drawers. When you shop, take along any tall or awkward items that you wash regularly to be sure they fit in the dishwasher before you buy it.

near-the-sink appliances

Used near—or in—the sink in conjunction with dishwashers, waste-disposal units and trash compactors are handy supplements that make cleanup speedier and life easier.

- **Waste-disposal units** are those handy devices that grind up organic wastes and flush them down the drain in the kitchen sink. Continuous-feed disposal units keep working as long as cold water is running and peelings, parings, and leftovers are being fed into them. Controlled by a switch on a nearby wall or cabinet, the continuous-feed disposal unit is the least expensive option. Batch-feed disposal units can grind up 1 to 2 quarts of waste at one time. They are controlled by a built-in switch that you activate by replacing the strainer on the drain. Batch-feed models are safer to use—and more expensive. Before you install either of the units, check local building codes.

- **Trash compactors,** which measure from 12 to 15 inches wide, are available as freestanding or under-counter models and are typically placed near the main sink or a secondary one. Trim kits are available to make this appliance blend with other cabinetry. They compress inorganic waste, such as cans, bottles, paper, plastic, and dry food waste to about a quarter of their original size, thus greatly reducing the amount of inorganic trash you have to handle. If you pay by the bag for waste removal, a trash compactor may be a wise investment. Some models offer a key-activated safety feature, toe-touch latch, and automatic deodorizer.

OPPOSITE Dishwasher drawers require fewer movements to open, load, and close, making cleanup a breeze.

ABOVE This built-in counter steamer is conveniently installed in the kitchen's center island.

RIGHT Unobtrusive wall panels hide chutes that send kitchen recyclables to their proper bins in a garage or basement.

smart wash

Some of the latest washer models feature antiallergy cycles that reduce dust mites and pet dander on fabrics.

the laundry area

You spend a lot of time in the kitchen, so why not do the laundry there, too? It makes a lot of sense—and it sure beats trudging up and down the basement steps for every load of wash. In a kitchen with generous dimensions, you'll probably have space for a washer and dryer (48 to 58 inches wide for full-size, side-by-side machines), but it's important that you locate them outside of the main food-preparation area so that they not impede traffic flow when in use. Allocate space, too, for laundry supplies. Front-loading models with a control panel on the front can be tucked under the countertop, thus blending them into the room and creating counter space for folding clothes or supplementing kitchen work space. Another good idea—select stackable units and build a cabinet to enclose them. Top-loaders will also fit into a good-size kitchen, but because they can't be slid under a counter, they are more likely to become eyesores, unless you can conceal them behind folding or pocket pantry doors that don't open into the work aisle. Also, consider a built-in ironing station that can be installed inside a cabinet.

OPPOSITE Side-by-side or stackable front-loading units are good choices for a kitchen laundry center.

LEFT This washer-dryer combination shares space with the kitchen pantry.

ABOVE A laundry room that's adjacent to a kitchen has matching countertop and flooring materials.

6

Sinks and Faucets

Today's kitchen sinks and faucets are making a bold design statement. While stainless steel endures as the most popular sink finish, there are more options to consider—bigger sizes, deeper bowls, new configurations, and colors and materials galore. There are also great new faucets with multiple spray features and accessories ranging from soap dispensers to water purification systems. Despite their glamour, sinks and faucets are still the workhorses of the kitchen, so make sure your choices look good and work hard.

- sinks
- faucets

In this unusual melding of form with function, an antique pot of hammered copper works beautifully as a kitchen sink.

sinks

Here's a helpful rule of thumb for choosing a kitchen sink—identify your practical needs first; then go for good looks. With so many choices you won't have to sacrifice one for the other. Another pointer comes from the National Kitchen & Bath Association (NKBA), an industry trade group: a standard 22 x 24-inch single-bowl sink is sufficient for kitchens that measure 150 square feet or less; for kitchens that are over that size, a larger single-bowl design or a double- or triple-bowl model are better choices.

If you haven't bought a kitchen sink for a while you'll be dazzled by your choices. And you may be surprised that many kitchens, even relatively modest ones, sport two or even three sinks. There's the primary one, located at the heart of the work area near the dishwasher and devoted to cleanup. There may also be a small prep sink, often located away from the busiest area and intended for a second cook or for a helpful dinner guest who may be washing or chopping vegetables or fruit. This secondary sink, a nice amenity for any household, is practically a necessity for a two-cook kitchen. If you have a large family or entertain often, you may want to install a bar sink that allows people to help themselves to beverages without getting in the cooks' way. If this auxiliary sink is accompanied by an undercounter refrigerator and enough counter space for a coffeemaker, you've got a beverage center.

Unless you select unusual shapes, super sizes, or deluxe materials such as natural stone, concrete, copper, brass, fire clay, or handmade ceramics, kitchen sinks are not especially big-ticket items. An investment of a couple of hundred dollars will get you a high-quality single- or double-bowl model in porcelain, stainless steel, or a composite material. The price could go up several hundred more for color, multiple bowls, or solid surfacing, and you'll pay another premium for apron-front farmhouse sinks no matter what the material.

OPPOSITE This integrated stainless-steel double sink contrasts with the butcher-block countertop.

ABOVE A small auxiliary sink is available for use by a second cook working at the island.

RIGHT This shallow prep sink with a self-draining bottom grid is ideal for rinsing fruits and vegetables.

LEFT In this traditional-style kitchen, the exposed-apron sink matches the warm metallic of the faucet.

RIGHT This brushed stainless-steel sink features a sculptural shape, elegant corners, and generous dimensions.

BELOW A smaller prep sink can be a handy complement to the main sink in the kitchen.

OPPOSITE BOTTOM Some of today's double-bowl sinks pair a large basin with a medium-size one, a useful configuration for many busy kitchens.

popular materials

When it's time to choose a kitchen sink, you can go for the glamour, selecting a material such as stone, hand-painted china, or even glass. But if you want to make a more conventional choice, there are some solid options for your consideration.

The familiar look of glossy white porcelain over cast iron has great appeal for many people, and this durable material is also available in myriad colors. Stains that may develop over time are generally easy to remove. A perfect match for trendy pro-style appliances, **stainless steel** is affordable, easy-care, and long lasting; 18- or 20-gauge steel promises durability and strength, and a satin finish disguises most water spots and scratches. Other metals, such as **copper** and **brass,** look great but require lots of care and polishing. Used alone or molded into a countertop, **solid surfacing** comes in many colors and stone-looks. It's pricey but requires little maintenance; the occasional scratch, dent, or stain can be successfully repaired. Often used for trendy farmhouse sinks, **concrete** and **soapstone** are costly but practically indestructible. Soapstone comes in several earthy colors, and concrete can be tinted any shade you like.

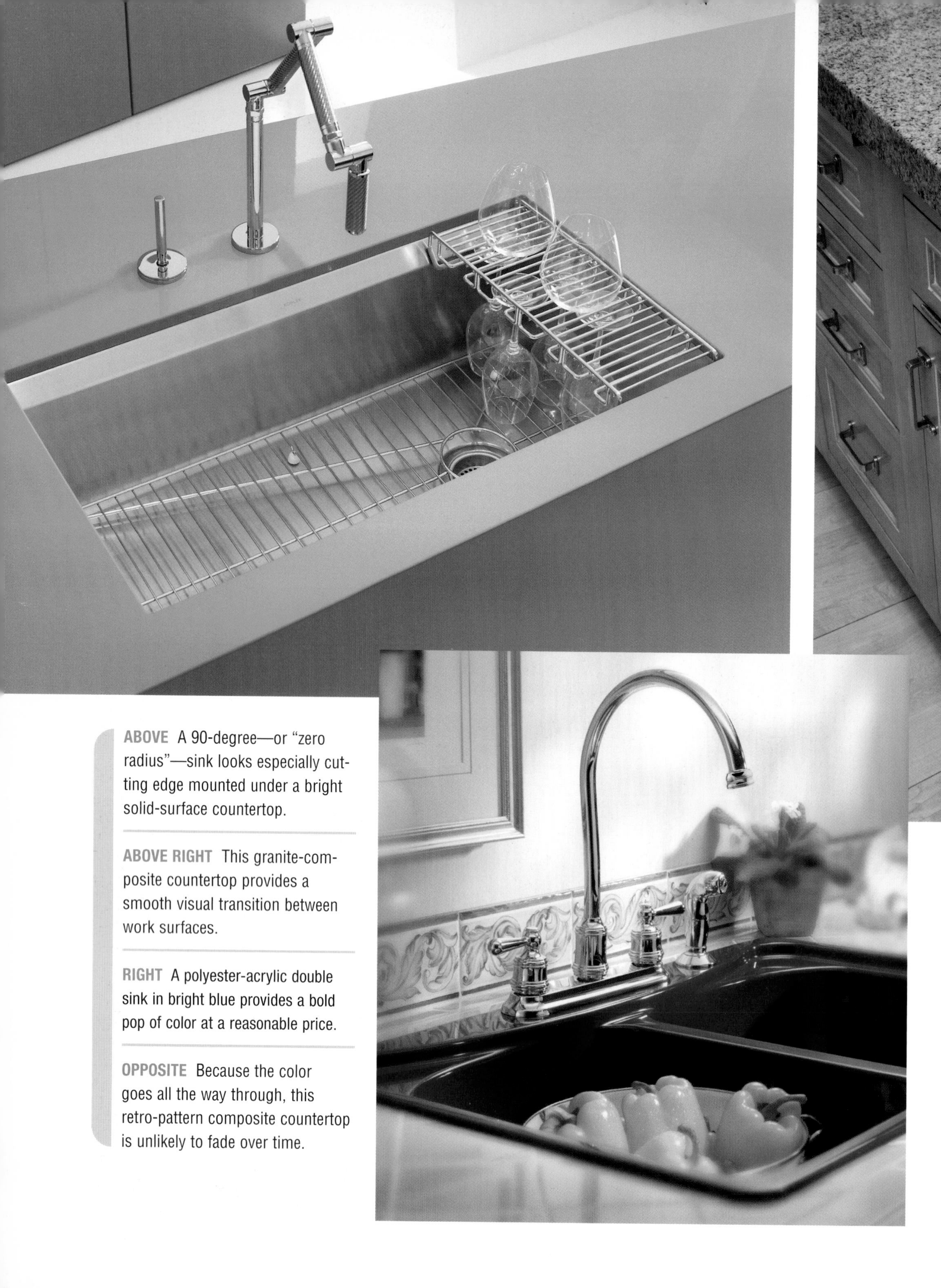

ABOVE A 90-degree—or "zero radius"—sink looks especially cutting edge mounted under a bright solid-surface countertop.

ABOVE RIGHT This granite-composite countertop provides a smooth visual transition between work surfaces.

RIGHT A polyester-acrylic double sink in bright blue provides a bold pop of color at a reasonable price.

OPPOSITE Because the color goes all the way through, this retro-pattern composite countertop is unlikely to fade over time.

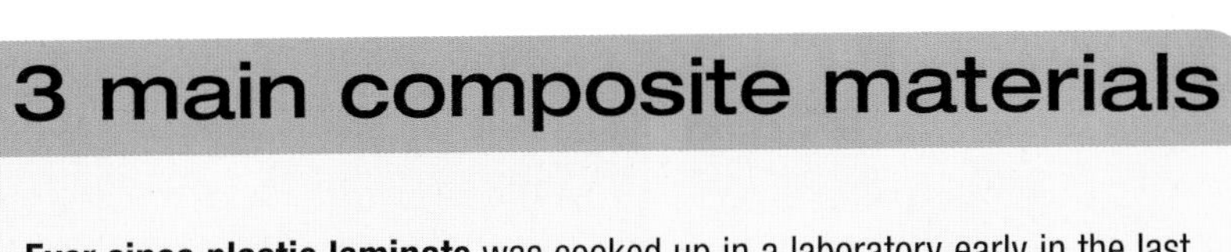

3 main composite materials

Ever since plastic laminate was cooked up in a laboratory early in the last century, product engineers have been working to create materials that supply the look and durability of stone but cost less. One case in point: composites, which are available in three basic types.

- **Polyester/acrylic** is the least expensive and least durable of the big three. It's somewhat soft, so it scratches and stains easily. Still, if your budget is tight, you'll like its price, glossy surface, and bright colors.

- **Quartz composite,** a mixture of crushed quartz and resin fillers, is durable and resistant to most stains and scratches. Its moderate price and earthy or bright colors, including a brilliant blue and zippy yellow, make it appealing.

- **Granite composite,** a mixture of crushed granite and resin fillers, is the most expensive—and most durable—of the composites, offering high resistance to chips, stains, scratches, and burns. It's available in a number of colors and in several neutrals.

Go Green

Look for composite countertops made of recycled glass suspended in cement, which do not release VOCs into the air.

installation styles

- **Self-rimming (drop-in) sinks** are the least costly and most common. Available in any material, they are set into the counter with the edges overlapping. The downside—crumbs, water splashes, other debris, and germs can collect along the seam of the rim.
- **Undermounted sinks** attach below the countertop. With no visible edges, they make a smooth transition between sink and counter. To avoid warping or buckling, choose a water-resistant counter material.
- **Integral sinks,** made of the same material as the counter, look seamless and sleek and provide no crevices where food can lodge. They can be fabricated of any moldable material, such as stainless steel, solid surfacing, composites, and concrete.
- **Exposed-apron sinks** are undermounted but reveal the sink's front panel. They can be made from most types of sink materials.

OPPOSITE TOP LEFT This under-mounted single-bowl kitchen sink is deep enough to accommodate whatever can fit in the oven.

OPPOSITE TOP RIGHT This humble farmhouse-style sink gets a sophisticated makeover in sleek black.

OPPOSITE BOTTOM A self-rimming sink in stainless steel features generously sized double bowls.

ABOVE The clean look of this contemporary kitchen is enhanced by the integral double sinks made of pure white solid-surfacing material.

LEFT This exposed apron-front sink in brushed stainless steel blends well with this kitchen's mix of styles.

LEFT Some of today's sinks can serve as full-fledged food-staging areas, which makes cleanup easy and saves counter space.

BOTTOM LEFT The trough sink is an idea borrowed from restaurants to accommodate several cooks or cooks' helpers at the same time.

BOTTOM RIGHT A double-bowl sink, such as this stainless-steel model, is usually sufficient to service a small kitchen.

OPPOSITE TOP This triple-bowl sink is a true workhorse, thanks to a small prep basin flanked by two medium-size bowls.

OPPOSITE BOTTOM This crescent-shaped sink's stainless-steel finish has a slightly warm undertone that meshes with the countertop.

take your pick of

single-, double-, or triple-bowl sinks

OPPOSITE This tiny marble vessel was cleverly installed in an antique dry sink.

LEFT A black finish and unusual shape give this prep sink a bold look that contrasts with the simple farm table.

BELOW Bar sinks are so small that you can afford to splurge a little with a fancy faucet set or a gleaming hammered-copper finish.

prep and bar sinks

In addition to the primary sink, which is the heart of the cleanup zone, prep and bar sinks are becoming standard equipment.

You'll welcome a prep sink if your kitchen is large, if two cooks often work together in it, or if you entertain frequently. Especially useful when two cooks are working simultaneously or when a dinner guest is pressed into service to scrub some vegetables or make a salad, prep sinks are placed away from the work zone. Typically drop-in or undermount models, they are small, ranging in size from 9-in. rounds to 18-in. squares, although some are smaller. Because such a diminutive sink doesn't represent a major investment or get hard use, you can splurge a little bit on sexy materials that wouldn't hold up well in the primary work area—gleaming copper or brass, or a hand-painted ceramic or glass bowl, for example.

The popularity of bar sinks is a direct result of the kitchen's current status as a living center. With one cook busy at the main sink and a helper or two using the prep sink, a third sink where hot or cold drinks can be served is often a necessity.

water log

Most homeowners spend around five hours per week at the sink, more than they do in front of the stove or the refrigerator.

how to choose a kitchen sink

It's tempting to put looks first, but give some thought to your day-to-day practical needs, too. If you have a dishwasher, a large single-bowl sink may be sufficient; add a prep sink if yours is a two-cook household—but only if you have space for it. No dishwasher? You'll need a double-bowl design with equal-size basins. Other double-bowl options include one large and one medium or one small bowl. A triple-bowl sink with two deep basins for washing and rinsing and a small basin is a good choice for a kitchen with no dishwasher and no space for a separate prep sink. If you entertain, a bar sink is a bonus.

Match the sink with the decor, too. Stainless steel, for example, looks good in a contemporary room, but it's also at home in any style kitchen, as are solid-surface and composite-stone designs. Porcelain sinks, in white or a pretty color, and copper sinks blend beautifully with traditional or country decors. Concrete or soapstone designs have a handsome quality. Depending on the other elements in the kitchen, they can look rustic or refined.

ABOVE LEFT A single-hole faucet with a swivel spout can easily service a two-bowl sink.

ABOVE A swan-neck spout is both graceful and practical—it allows plenty of clearance for tall pots.

OPPOSITE This integral, zero-radius sink is a kitchen star thanks to its unusual size, shape, color, and material.

standard sizes

SINK DIMENSIONS (in inches)

Sink Type	Width	Front to Rear	Basin Depth
Single-bowl	25	21–22	8–9
Double-bowl	33, 36	21–22	8–9
Side-disposal	33	21–22	8–9, 7
Triple-bowl	43	21–22	8, 6, 10
Corner	17–18 (each way)	21–11	8–9
Bar	15–25	15	5½–6

LEFT Gleaming chrome fittings pair wonderfully with gray-streaked white marble.

BELOW This faucet's earthy finish complements both traditional and contemporary kitchens.

OPPOSITE TOP This high-arch faucet adds both practicality and panache.

OPPOSITE BOTTOM A clean-lined, wall-mounted stainless-steel faucet harmonizes with this stainless-steel sink.

faucets

Like kitchen sinks, today's faucets have a lot of panache. But for the moment, overlook their luxurious finishes and interesting shapes, and focus on their construction. Faucets have to work hard, and you might as well buy one that will stand up well to daily wear and tear. Before you fall in love with a particular design, find out about its inner construction. The best-quality faucets are made of solid brass or a brass-base material, which are corrosion resistant. Valve construction is important as well. Ball valves ensure good quality in single-lever models, while ceramic-disk valves make single- and dual-lever faucets reliable and long lasting. Avoid faucets that use washers and plastic parts. Although these products are cheaper initially, they will cost you in repairs and eventual replacement. Investigate finishes, too, and choose the ones that have a warranty, typically 10 years.

Faucets with pullout spray heads are so popular today that they constitute a bona fide kitchen trend. Other favorite built-in features may include spouts that swivel 180 degrees, antiscald mechanisms, and water filtration systems. More options, such as side-mounted sprayers, soap dispensers, and instant hot-water dispensers, are installed separately. Don't select these accessories willy-nilly. First, ask yourself if this is a feature you will really use; then make sure it matches the style and finish of your faucets and the number of holes predrilled in your sink deck. Often overlooked is the strainer and drain assembly, which you will probably have to buy separately.

installation styles

- **Center-set** fittings require only one drilled hole. They combine a spout and two handles set in a single base about 4 in. apart center to center. They are the least expensive installation type.
- **Widespread** fittings require three holes and appear to consist of three separate pieces. More costly than centersets, these sets place hot and cold handles 8 to 12 in. apart center to center, with the spout in between.
- **Single-hole** fittings condense the spout and one handle for both hot and cold water into one unit.
- **Deck-mounted** faucets are installed on the rim of the sink or into the counter around it.
- **Wall-mounted** faucets are installed into the wall directly above the basin or, in the case of potfillers, above the cooktop. (See page 163.)

OPPOSITE TOP This wide-spread faucet set has separate hot- and cold-water valves and a side-mounted sprayer.

OPPOSITE BOTTOM LEFT This sleek stainless-steel model offers a built-in water filter and detachable sprayer.

OPPOSITE BOTTOM RIGHT The satin-bronze finish on this gooseneck design supplies a soft patina.

RIGHT This single-lever faucet with a detachable spray head is finished in subtle satin nickel.

BELOW A deck-mounted, wide-spread fitting in gleaming polished chrome is a reproduction of a Victorian-era model.

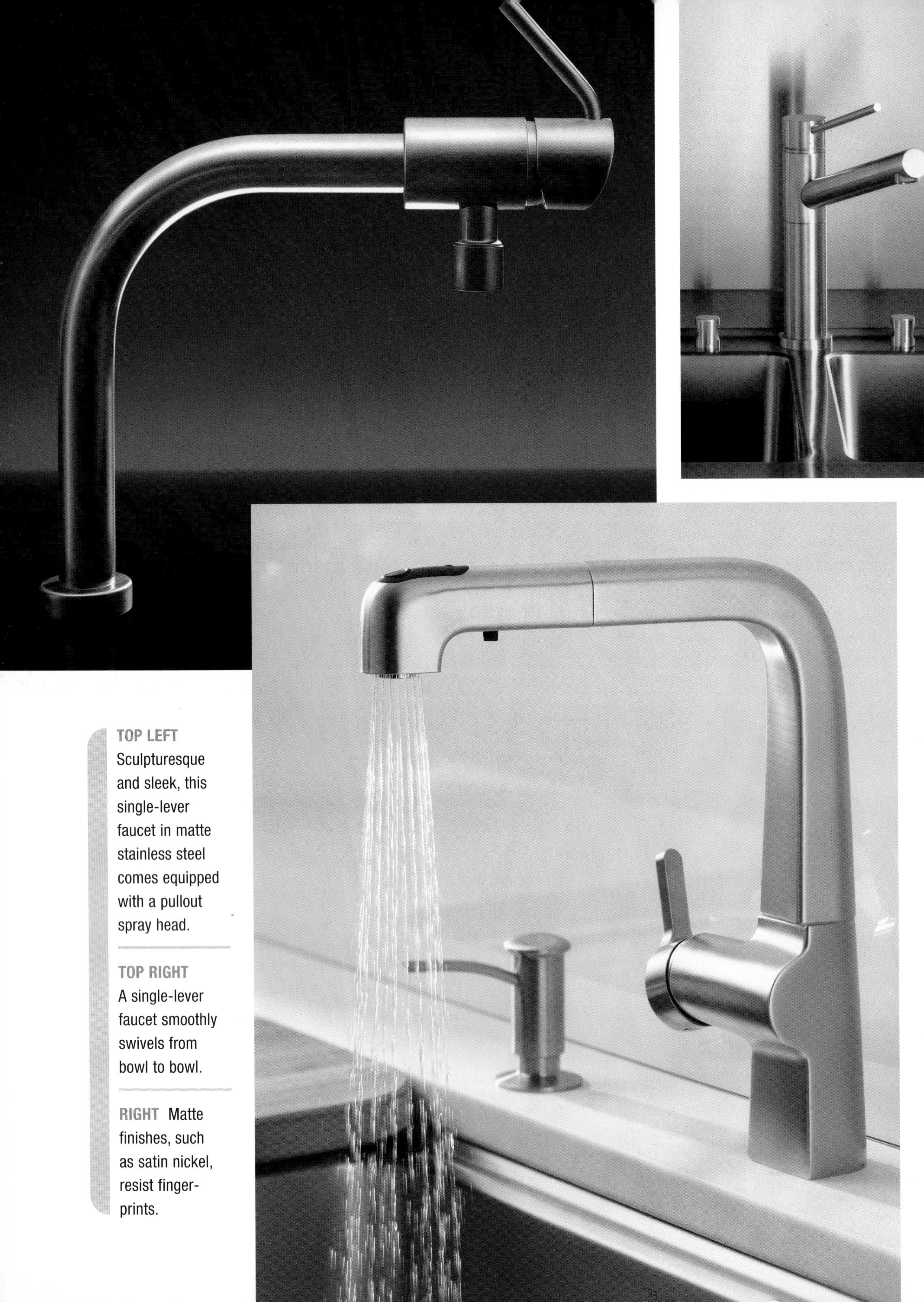

TOP LEFT Sculpturesque and sleek, this single-lever faucet in matte stainless steel comes equipped with a pullout spray head.

TOP RIGHT A single-lever faucet smoothly swivels from bowl to bowl.

RIGHT Matte finishes, such as satin nickel, resist fingerprints.

ABOVE Matte nickel has a glamorous gleam. It's suitable for vintage fittings or for the more contemporary style shown here.

RIGHT A design resembling a water pump has an antique French flavor that would nicely suit an Old World or traditional kitchen setting.

shop smart for shapes and styles

Today's handsome kitchen faucets are artful, resembling little kitchen sculptures. Some are dramatically contemporary, others charmingly vintage, and yet many belong to no specific design category. To maintain design unity, choose a faucet that coordinates with the overall look of your kitchen. Some will blend with elements from any style, but an ultrasleek model will look wrong amidst the coziness of a country kitchen, and vice versa. Here are other things to consider before you buy:

- **Handle Style.** Two-handle fittings are widely available, but single handles are more effective for controlling water temperature and pressure. Lever-style or wrist-blade handles are the easiest to operate because you don't have to grip them.
- **Spout Style.** Many designs have a standard spout that's a bit higher than the faucet base. But most people seem to prefer high-arc spouts, available in traditional or contemporary styles, because they allow clearance for large pots and platters. Some types swivel to reach both bowls in a two-basin sink.
- **Budget.** You can buy a faucet for under a hundred dollars, but for high quality and more options you'll need to spend at least two or three times that much. Prices rise to about $1,000 for special finishes and features.
- **Compatibility.** Buy your sink and faucets at the same time and from the same source to make sure they are compatible. Never assume faucets will fit the sink you have chosen unless your salesperson or designer has verified it.

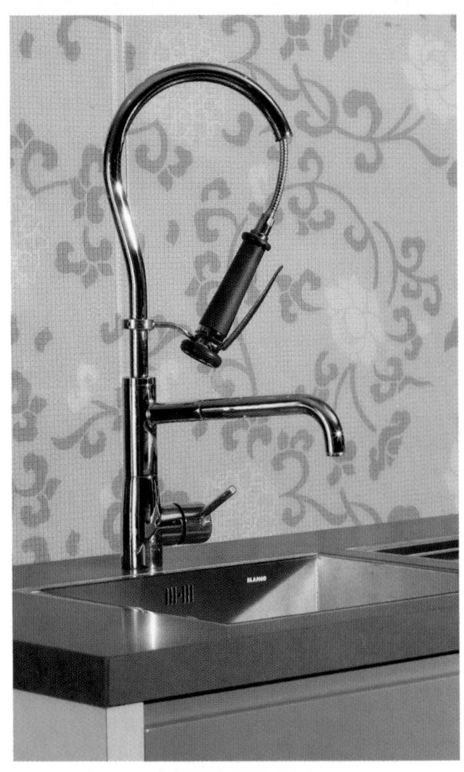

pot fillers and sprayers

- **Pot fillers,** borrowed from restaurant kitchens, have been a favorite feature of really serious cooks for some time, but now almost everybody wants one. These handy fittings are mounted on the wall above the range or cooktop, and they allow cooks to fill large pots with water at the site rather than lugging them, heavy and spilling over, from sink to burner. They are typically single-lever models that supply only cold water. Most of them are double-jointed, which means that they extend to reach all burners, then fold back flat against the wall when not in use. The best models have a handle at the spout as well as at the wall so that the user doesn't have to lean over hot burners to open or close the valve.

- **Sprays,** handy for rinsing dishes, produce, and the sink basin, come in two types. **Side sprays** are sold separately and mounted next to the faucet. **Built-in, pullout,** or **pull-down faucets** have a retractable hose and offer a high-volume spray. Hoses made of stainless steel offer the smoothest operation.

TOP LEFT With the hose clipped to the base, this fitting functions as a faucet.

LEFT This single-lever model is finished in satin nickel.

ABOVE This oil-rubbed copper fitting pivots to fill pots, then folds back neatly against the wall.

OPPOSITE This pot filler swivels to accommodate more than one burner.

warming trend

Oil-rubbed bronze works well not only with antique-style fittings but also with retro and transitional looks.

hot finishes

There was a time when kitchen faucets were almost exclusively made of chrome. That serviceable material is still a good choice in terms of durability, tarnish resistance, and economy. But many other finishes have arrived on the scene in recent years. If you are willing to part with a little more money—and spend a little more time on maintenance—you can add a great deal of design splash to your kitchen sink.

The hot finish these days is **stainless steel,** partly because it is a good match for ever-popular pro-style appliances. It is also extremely durable and looks good with any style of faucet, contemporary or traditional. Exuding a decidedly warm, old-fashioned look, **oil-rubbed bronze, matte-finished brass,** and **antique copper** are also increasing in popularity and are considered a good complement to an Old World decor. They also pair well with stone and concrete elements. **Brass** is a perennial favorite. **Baked-on epoxy** finishes, available in a wide variety of bright colors and neutrals, can add a note of cheer to casual country-style kitchens; a black epoxy finish, on the other hand, goes with everything and coordinates well with stainless steel and black appliances.

Satin or brushed finishes are preferred nowadays for practical and aesthetic reasons—they don't show the fingerprints and water spots that mar high-gloss faucets.

OPPOSITE The warm finish of this farmhouse-style faucet looks fabulous with wood.

RIGHT For a traditional kitchen, this satin-brass faucet has a period look.

BELOW LEFT Polished copper has a glamorous gleam.

BELOW RIGHT The rubbed-bronze finish is a good match for this natural stone countertop.

BOTTOM Polished chrome has been a popular faucet finish since the turn of the century.

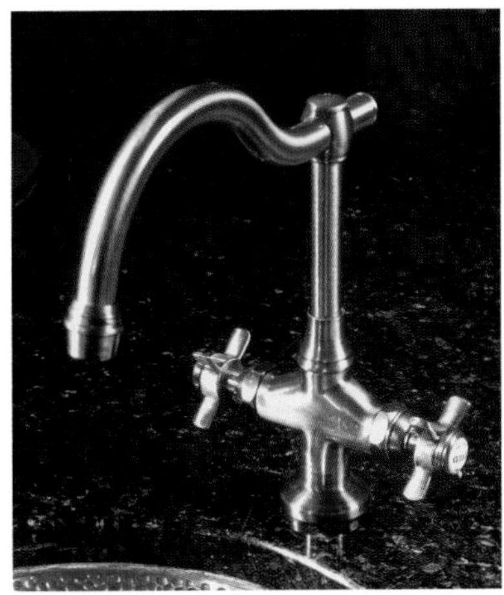

7

Countertops

Both a design element and a work surface, the countertop is an important kitchen feature. Making a choice can be daunting—there are many options that are appealing, durable, and cleanable, although some are higher-maintenance than others. If you're a serious cook, you may want a tough surface that doesn't need a lot of care. If your countertops will be a major design feature, it makes sense to look for a material that commands attention.

- **stone**
- **solid-surfacing material**
- **specialty surfaces**
- **plastic laminate**
- **concrete**
- **wood and metal**

The rich, cocoa-and-white granite countertops lend warmth and distinction to this simple, sunny kitchen.

UNGT.
UNGT.
UNGT.
10%

stone

If you're considering a stone countertop, you already know that **granite** has reigned supreme for quite some time. Beautiful and luminous, it makes a strong design statement and looks great in traditional or contemporary kitchens. Although granite is the hardest, most durable, and least scratchable of the stones, it is porous and stains easily. To maintain its luminosity, you must seal it right after installation and reseal it often. Granite is expensive, and it's heavy, requiring more support than standard cabinet framing provides. **Marble,** another beautiful stone, is seldom used on serious work counters because oils, tomatoes, and other acidic substances readily stain its porous surface. Instead, use it in a baking area, where its cool surface is ideal for rolling dough, or in another part of your kitchen that doesn't see much action. Frequent sealing helps prevent stains, but most people aren't willing to do that much maintenance. Like marble, **limestone** is soft and susceptible to staining, but homeowners are choosing it anyway. Seduced by its creamy-beige tones and weathered-looking surface, some people like the character that comes with imperfection.

Slate is durable, less porous, and requires no sealing. It's available in black, gray, and shades of green and red. Like all stone, it looks luxurious but can scratch and chip easily. **Soapstone** is enjoying a resurgence. It stands up to heavy use and ages to a charcoal gray.

OPPOSITE This impressively hefty countertop is made of Jura yellow limestone.

LEFT The coolness of marble makes it a perfect surface for rolling dough, but it must be protected from cuts.

BELOW Granite, the king of countertops, is revered for its distinctive variations of color and pattern.

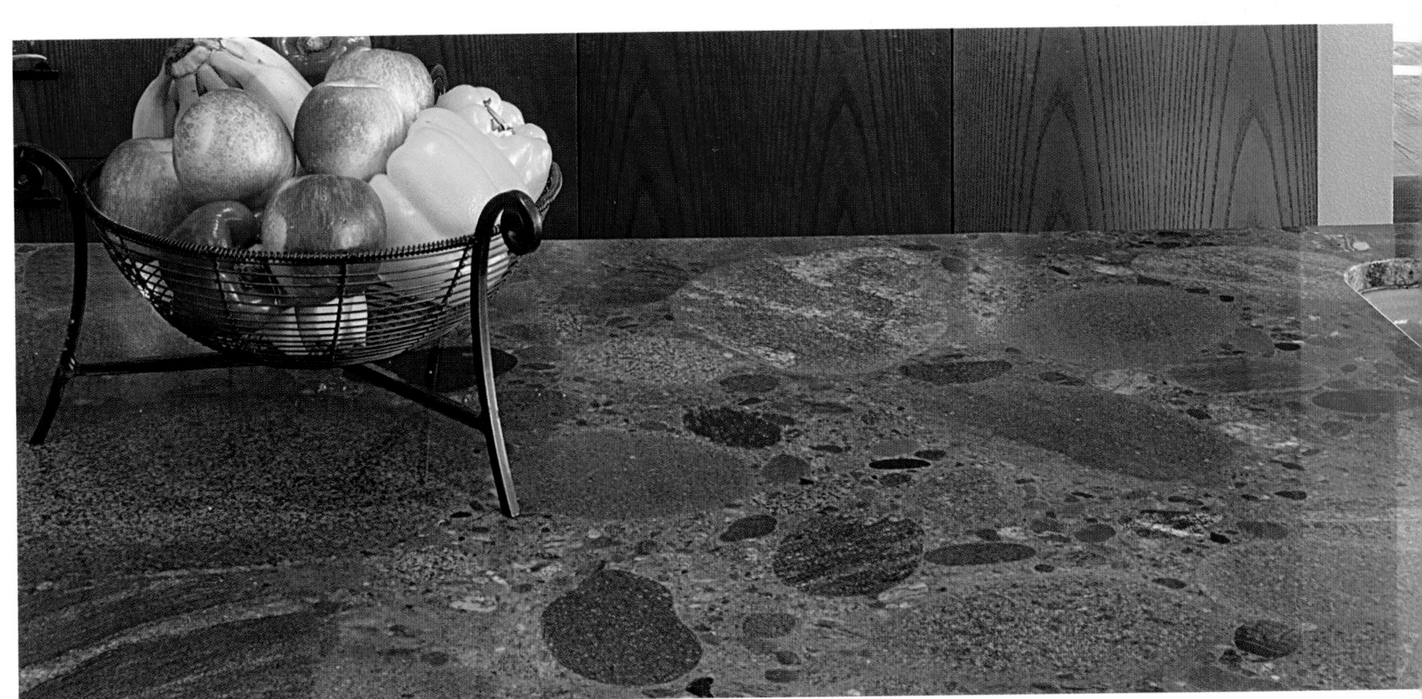

engineered (composite) stone

Produced by binding stone chips—predominantly quartz—to powders and resins, engineered or man-made stone (also called composite material) is an extremely hard and durable material that has become a popular choice for kitchen counters. Because they are nonporous, engineered stone products require less maintenance than granite and don't need to be sealed periodically. Their impervious surfaces also provide more stain and bacterial resistance than granite.

Many engineered products offer a speckled or variegated look that somewhat resembles natural stone without the random swirls or color variations. Like granite, engineered stone comes in 52-in. by 120-in. slabs; countertop fabricators cut and shape the material.

Several companies manufacture engineered stone in a variety of colors and finishes. And while it's almost as expensive as the real thing, it may be worth the cost if you're after low maintenance and a more uniform look.

tough stuff

Because engineered stone is stronger than granite, edges are cleaner, allowing for easier sealing of seams.

BELOW This island is fabricated from a quartz-composite product that evokes the look of limestone.

OPPOSITE The striking countertop in this designer kitchen is a new composite product containing hand-cut semiprecious stones.

Considerably less expensive than natural stone or composite materials, solid surfacing is a man-made, nonporous product. Made of filled acrylic and polyester polymers, the material can be used to form a countertop with an integral sink for an elegant seamless appearance. It can also be carved and finished with interesting architectural edges. (See "Edge Treatments," opposite.) For an especially distinguished look, solid-surface countertop edges can be inlaid with wood, metal, or a contrasting color strip. Another attractive feature of the material is the wide variety of colors and patterns that are available. The stone look-alikes are the best known, but solid-surfacing material also comes in a variety of whites, pastels, primary colors, and earth tones. It resists stains, moisture, and stands up well to wear and tear. Solid-surfacing countertops are easy to clean with abrasive cleansers, but they are not impervious to burns or scratches. Fortunately, because the color goes all the way through the material, these marks can be buffed or sanded out. It is best to trust this process to a professional. The cost of solid-surface countertops can be comparable to some stones, although certain colors are more affordable.

solid-surfacing material

on-the-go

Cutting-edge mobile workshops can visit a site, fabricate the countertop, and install it in about one day.

OPPOSITE Because it is man-made, solid-surfacing material offers a great diversity of colors and textures.

TOP RIGHT The product features hundreds of looks, from speckles of granite to the swirls of a marble vein.

ABOVE Unlike a veneer, color and pattern are consistent throughout solid-surfacing material, and finishes range from matte to high gloss.

edge treatments

Select an edge treatment for your countertop that matches the kitchen's architectural style.

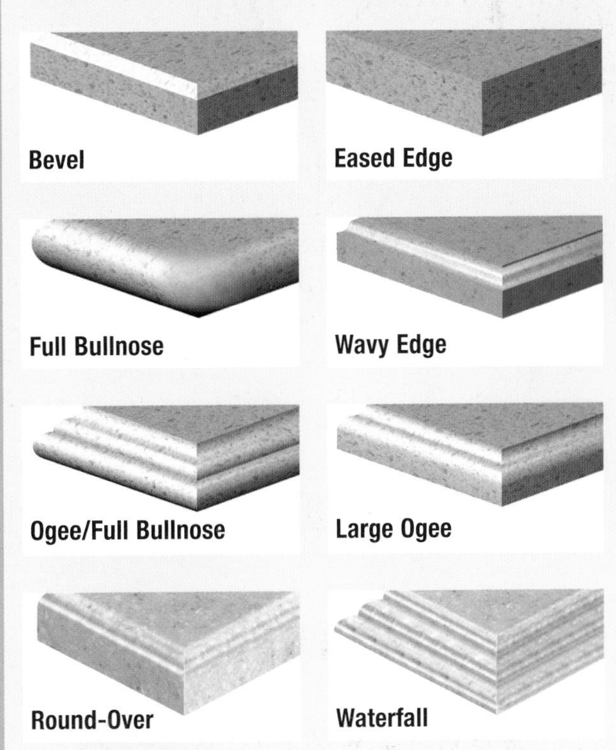

ABOVE This countertop was crafted of more than 10,000 marble tiles.

RIGHT Individually cut semiprecious stones glow in this stone countertop.

OPPOSITE TOP This counter is made of recycled glass.

OPPOSITE BOTTOM Concrete tiles can be less costly than custom-poured designs.

Go Green

Surfaces made from recycled materials satisfy both the designer's eye and the homeowner's conscience.

specialty surfaces

There are hundreds of exciting new countertop fabrications on the market these days, many the result of consumer demand for products that are attractive, don't waste precious resources, and are healthy for the home and the environment. Two products on the cutting edge of countertop materials are recycled glass mixed with concrete and recycled paper. Both products are petroleum-free, durable, heat-resistant, and surprisingly beautiful.

Natural stone meets most green criteria and is still a top choice for many homeowners. However, granite has loosened its grip on the top rung recently, making room for some less-common options, such as marble, soapstone, and limestone. These natural beauties were once thought to be too fragile for heavy kitchen use, but greatly improved sealers have now made them much easier to maintain. Another new counter trend is to combine two textures of the same stone, such as a sandblasted surface near the sink and a smooth gloss finish on a center-island snack area.

For homeowners seeking a bright splash of color on their counters, engineered stone is a great option. Eco-friendly quartz composite comes in a range of colors not found in natural stone, including lime green, orange, and royal blue.

TOP LEFT The cheerful hues in this mosaic-tile backsplash set the tone for the kitchen's color scheme.

RIGHT Running this taupe subway-tile backsplash along the entire wall imparts a sense of visual continuity.

LEFT It is easy to install a backsplash yourself without disturbing other elements in the kitchen.

BOTTOM LEFT The light-reflecting reds and golds of this mosaic-tile wall resemble hundreds of tiny jewels.

BOTTOM RIGHT This glass-tile backsplash in a retro color palette lends distinction to the range area.

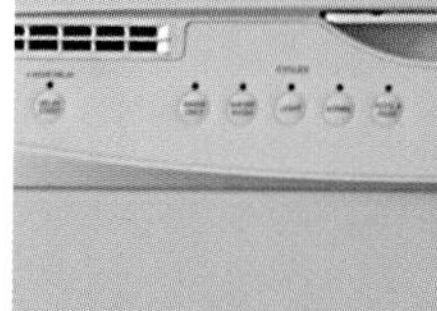

a gallery of backsplashes

Backsplashes have come a long way, from insignificant little shields that protected the walls behind the sink and cooktop to significant design elements. And because the space they occupy is proportionately small, you can afford to splurge a little, selecting a luxurious material that might be too pricey or too delicate to use in larger doses. If you're after a unified look, you can continue the countertop material right up the backsplash. Looking for a little more excitement? Try tile laid out in an interesting pattern. In some kitchens, the cooktop backsplash is devoted to an elaborate tile mural. Want more razzle-dazzle? Choose shiny copper, retro-style quilted stainless steel, shimmering glass tiles, sections of mirror, or a mix of materials. In a family-oriented kitchen, cork backsplashes furnish a place to tack recipes, family photos, mementos, messages, and the like. The sky's the limit, but stick with an easy-to-clean material behind the sink and cooktop—spatters and splashes are inevitable.

like a stone

Drawing on technology developed for flooring, new laminate countertops bear a striking resemblance to natural stone.

plastic laminate

Unless you choose a fancy edge treatment—a contrasting color, a bevel, or a wood or metal inlay—plastic laminate is your best bet for kitchen-counter economy. Other positive aspects of this versatile material include quick and straightforward installation, easy cleanup, and an infinite variety of colors, textures, and patterns, including stone, wood, and metal look-alikes. A new plastic-laminate pattern designed to mimic ceramic tile comes complete with indentations that resemble grout lines. But you'll have to be careful not to stain, scorch, chip, or scratch this material. These blemishes cannot be satisfactorily repaired. And you'll need to be vigilant about water, too—don't let it collect, especially near seams where it can warp or cause the material to lift off its substrate. However, plastic laminate comes in different grades and is usually affordable to replace. A post-formed countertop, which comes with an integral backsplash and a rounded edge, is even more economical. The color selection for these ready-made counters is limited and the laminate is thinner, so it's more susceptible to damage. But you will get a few good years out of it—and the price is right. Keep in mind that spots stand out sharply on a high-gloss plastic laminate; matte or textured finishes do a better job of camouflaging everyday wear and tear.

OPPOSITE Plastic laminates are impact-resistant, nonporous, and unlike stone, warm to the touch.

ABOVE RIGHT The newest laminate products offer the luxurious look and texture of stone at an affordable price.

RIGHT You can order a plastic-laminate counter built to your specifications, such as this wood-edge treatment.

concrete

concrete is

Once considered daring and avant-garde, concrete counters have moved into the mainstream. And it's no wonder—concrete is an eco-friendly alternative to petroleum-based synthetic products and nonrenewable natural resources, such as quarried stone. It's also an intriguing and versatile material that can be formed into any number of interesting shapes. It's a natural choice for an integral counter-and-sink installation, and it can be personalized with curves and angles, sparkly glass chips, and even personal mementos, such as bits of broken dishware, seashells, or leaf imprints.

Concrete is often used in its natural state, a gray hue that mellows over time. If that look reminds you too much of a sidewalk or a garage floor, try a tint customized to your color scheme. Any number of hues are available from earthy tones to vivid and deeply saturated shades. Finishes vary from highly textured to rough or rustic, glossy and polished to subdued and low sheen.

Concrete counters are resistant to heat and scratching, but because they are porous, they can stain readily and require periodic sealing. All of this versatility and uniqueness comes with a high price tag. Concrete itself is not expensive, but fabrication is difficult and time consuming and requires an expert. If poorly or hastily prepared, your concrete counter will surely crack. It's a good idea to get references from the installer and check out previous installations that have been in place for some time.

natural and has a warm, tactile quality

OPPOSITE TOP Some concrete countertops are cast on site in molds built to the customer's specifications.

OPPOSITE BOTTOM This substantial concrete counter adds pleasing heft and balance to the center island.

ABOVE Because each concrete countertop is hand cast, it exhibits subtle variations in color and texture.

ABOVE The satin finish on these sleek stainless-steel countertops helps resist fingerprints and hide scratches and abrasions.

BOTTOM LEFT Wood adds a warmth and beauty to this kitchen island that no other material can match.

BOTTOM RIGHT Unusual zebra wood, prized for its black and brown stripes, is certified as a sustainable resource.

OPPOSITE TOP The expanse of stainless steel atop the L-shaped island gives this kitchen the feel of a professional kitchen.

OPPOSITE BOTTOM Butcher block is a beautiful and no-fuss counter choice, especially if you love to cook and entertain.

wood and metal

Despite its vulnerability to moisture, scratches, and stains, wood, especially butcher block, remains popular. Its warm look is particularly suitable for country or traditional kitchens. Hardwood counters are easy to work on and relatively easy to maintain. Pools of water will do damage, however, if not wiped up right away. Your wood counter will eventually show stains and scratches. Some cooks like this well-used look, but if you don't agree you can periodically sand out imperfections and reseal the wood with nontoxic mineral oil. On the other hand, bamboo is durable (harder than maple) and eco-friendly.

Wood is a sanitary material with inherent properties that protect it from built-up bacteria. Metal is also sanitary, and the only countertop material that can be safely cleaned with bleach. A great addition to a trendy pro-style kitchen or a minimalist design, metal counters—usually stainless steel—are popular options. Stainless steel is impervious to heat, water, and stains. It can be formed into an integral sink and countertop configuration and is extremely durable (the lower the gauge, the thicker the material). On the down side, it's expensive and noisy to work on unless it's cushioned with extra plywood. A satin or brushed finish can disguise some of the scratches that come with time and use.

8

Lighting

Whether you're remodeling an old kitchen or building a new one, abundant light should be high on the list of the features you will incorporate. Without it, a kitchen isn't pleasant, efficient, or safe. In fact, lack of light is one of the reasons homeowners decide to remodel. So why do many people often fail to plan for it? Tackle the question now, while you are still in the planning stages. As you will see, there are many ways to introduce natural and artificial light to make your kitchen shine with style.

- **natural light**
- **artificial light**

During daytime hours, sunlight streams into this contemporary kitchen through several types of windows.

natural light

A single window over the sink and a pane of glass in the top half of the back door—sound familiar? Until recently, this scenario represented the extent of natural lighting in many kitchens. Fortunately, that picture has changed. Nowadays, architects, interior designers, and remodeling contractors are well versed in window technology and can help you bring abundant natural light into your new kitchen and establish a connection with the outdoors, too. If you're starting from scratch, plan the windows early in the process, when you are laying out the food-preparation and eating zones. If you're remodeling, look for ways to enlarge existing windows or seek out likely places to install new ones. Replacing dated windows with larger, more interesting units can introduce more light and at the same time make the kitchen more appealing. You might also consider adding windows or glass doors that overlook the garden, or installing a greenhouse window above the sink to supply sunshine and a spot to grow herbs year-round.

Before you commit to any new windows, ask yourself two questions. One, what kind of view will they provide? If you won't be looking at something pleasant, try a different location or consider a skylight, which maximizes sunlight but circumvents unattractive views. Two, will your new windows harmonize with the architecture of the house?

OPPOSITE Pouring in through a contemporary patio door, sunshine brightens up a dining area.

LEFT This large Palladian-style window delivers ample light and gorgeous views.

ABOVE Sunlight streaming through the French doors and windows creates a lovely pattern.

skylights and roof windows

According to some lighting experts, skylights supply up to 30 percent more light than vertical windows; and they also make the room feel larger.

Skylights, installed along a roof slope or on a flat roof, are generally not reachable. However, venting, or operable, skylights, hinged at the top, can be opened by an electric wall switch, motorized or manual hand-crank, or remote control device to provide fresh air and ventilation and to let hot summer air escape. Fixed skylights do not open.

Roof windows (the term is sometimes used interchangeably with operable skylight) are generally set lower in the roofline than skylights and are reachable. Sashes are designed to pivot so that the outside glass can be cleaned from inside the house.

To save money on energy bills, choose skylights and roof windows with insulated thermal glass, which will minimize heat loss in winter and cut down on heat gain in summer. Another way to combat heat gain is to shade skylights during the hottest part of the day. Skylight manufacturers offer blinds and shades as accessories. Using skylights with tinted glass is another way to reduce heat gain.

OPPOSITE High windows and ceiling beams create an ever-changing interplay of light and shadow.

ABOVE LEFT The slope of a cathedral ceiling is an ideal location for a room-brightening skylight.

ABOVE RIGHT To eliminate the risk of water damage, install flashing made specifically for your skylights.

RIGHT Tinted glass in your skylights or roof windows will shield your cabinetry from the direct sunlight.

nifty fixture

Pendant fixtures with retractable cords can stay above it all for overall lighting or move close for cozy dining.

artificial light

To create a welcoming—and safe—environment in your kitchen you will need artificial lighting in three categories. General, or ambient, lighting creates a comfortable level of brightness without being obvious about it—like a woman whose makeup is applied skillfully: she looks good but you can't pinpoint exactly why. Task lighting, crucial for efficiency and safety, should be installed everywhere there is close work done in the kitchen. Many people overlook accent lighting, but it, too, is important. By focusing attention on particular elements, say a shelf of pretty collectibles, you'll enhance the appeal of your kitchen. The bulbs you choose are also important. Incandescent bulbs emit a warm light. They don't cost much initially but eat up energy and generate heat. A more energy-efficient choice, warm-white fluorescent bulbs cast a shadowless, diffuse light, render colors and textures accurately, and are effective for general or task lighting. Halogen bulbs produce a whiter, brighter light. They are costly, however, and even the low-voltage type burn hotly and emit UV rays. New krypton and xenon bulbs are cooler, brighter, and most efficient.

fixture types

- **Suspended** globes, chandeliers, and pendants can light up an entire a room or a particular task area. Hang them 12–20 in. below an 8-ft. ceiling or 30–36 in. above the tops of tables and counters.

- **Surface-mount** fixtures attach directly to the ceiling or wall (sconces). Most distribute very even, shadowless general lighting. To minimize glare, surface-mount fixtures should be shielded. Fixtures with sockets for several smaller bulbs distribute more even lighting than those with just one or two large bulbs.

- **Recessed** fixtures are mounted inside the ceiling or soffit. They include fixed and aimable incandescent downlights, shielded fluorescent tubes, and totally luminous ceilings. Recessed fixtures require up to twice as much wattage as surface-mount and suspended types.

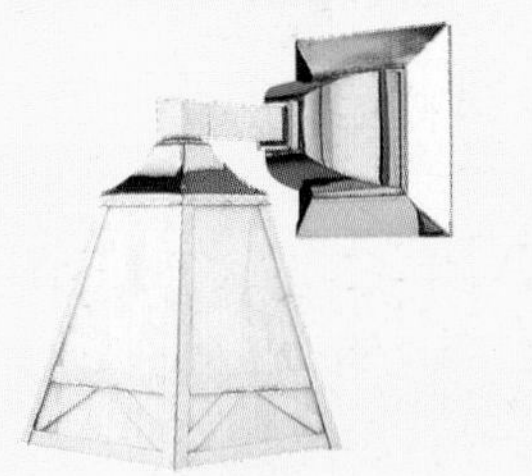

- **Track** lights, including bendable cable systems, can be used for general, task, or accent lighting—or any combination of the three. You can select from a broad array of modular fixtures, clip them anywhere along a track, and revise your lighting scheme any time you like. Locate tracks 12–24 in. out from the edges of wall cabinets to minimize shadows on countertops.

- **Undercabinet** compact fluorescent strips or incandescent fixtures mounted to the undersides of wall cabinets can bathe counters with sufficient task lighting. It's important to illuminate at least two-thirds of the counter's length.

- **Cove** lights reflect upward to the ceiling, creating smooth and even general lighting or dramatic architectural effects. Consider locating custom cove lights on top of wall cabinets in the space normally occupied by soffits.

OPPOSITE Sleek pendants provide warm light for dining.

LEFT This chandelier combines ambient and decorative lighting in a single fixture.

RIGHT Stylish glass pendants look great when grouped together.

general lighting

General, or ambient, lighting fills your entire kitchen, creating a warm and welcoming backdrop, both day and night. No matter how much natural light pours in, you will have to supplement it electrically on cloudy days; a well-balanced lighting scheme will duplicate the sunny glow of daylight. Sources for ambient light include ceiling fixtures, cabinet uplights, recessed downlights, wall sconces, even table lamps. Whatever your light sources, equip them with dimming features so that you can adjust brightness levels. You'll want bright light for working and seeing into cabinets and drawers, and softer, cozier illumination for dining. In today's open-plan homes, dimmers are also handy for coordinating kitchen lighting with adjacent rooms such as dining or living spaces or family rooms. Some lighting specialists even recommend that every light in the kitchen have its own circuit, which allows you to create the ambiance you want by adjusting lights individually. Space your fixtures so that they supply an even spread of light. If illumination breaks into a discernable pattern, you'll know that the light sources are placed too far apart.

Your color scheme will affect your lighting choices, as will the size and shape of the room. Light-colored or high-gloss cabinets, counters, and other surfaces reflect light, requiring less illumination than a room with dark or matte-finished surfaces. With high ceilings you'll need bright lights to dispel shadows. With lower ceilings, it's best to reduce brightness because light bounces off low ceilings and walls. The number of windows and the way they are oriented will also affect your lighting requirements.

Keep style in mind when you shop for fixtures. Recessed downlights, which are unobtrusive, will fit with any design scheme, but suspended fixtures, sconces, and track lights should match the look of your room. You'll have a wealth of designs from which to choose. Finishes for fixtures run the gamut, from enameled colors to shiny, matte, and antiqued metal patinas.

OPPOSITE LEFT New chromatherapy lighting can be altered to create a mood.

ABOVE CENTER This well-lit kitchen uses layers of light from several sources.

ABOVE RIGHT Recessed halogen lights keep this kitchen daytime bright.

RIGHT Multiple ceiling mounted fixtures cast a warm glow.

BELOW Ideal placement of task lighting is between a person's head and the work surface, which is why undercabinet lighting is so effective.

RIGHT A row of low-voltage xenon lights installed underneath the cabinets illuminates the work area in this kitchen.

OPPOSITE The halogen spots under this contemporary range hood provide bright light over the cooking surface.

lighting work areas

Any work you do in the kitchen—slicing, sautéing, rinsing, washing, even reading recipes or the newspaper—requires at least 100 watts of incandescent (or 60 watts of fluorescent) light. For countertop work areas, undercabinet lighting is the most effective. This type of light, whether fluorescent strips, miniature track lights, or a low-voltage linear system, should be installed close to the front edge of the wall cabinet so that it will bathe your counters in the kind of bright light you need for close work. The cooking and cleanup zones will also need effective task lighting. Undercabinet strips or recessed downlights are often used to illuminate the sink, and some range hoods come with built-in lighting for the cooktop. Track lighting, recessed fixtures, or pendants are popular choices to brighten work islands. If you will be using recessed ceiling fixtures or spots to light a work counter, place them 2 ft. away from the wall—otherwise you'll be standing in your own shadow while you work.

Does your kitchen include an eating area? If so, dim the undercabinet lighting, or turn it off completely when it's time to eat so that it doesn't shine right into people's eyes. Another tip—install a separate switch for each task light so that you can turn them off whenever you like.

Go Green

LED, which stands for "light-emitting diode," is a lighting technology that is long-lasting and extremely energy-efficient.

pendants and chandeliers

In the kitchen, pendants and chandeliers can supply all three types of lighting—overall, task, and accent—but they're most often used for ambient light over the dining table, a booth, an island, or any place family and friends gather to have their meals. If your kitchen ceiling is a conventional 8 ft. high, lighting specialists suggest that your suspended fixture be installed so that the bottom hangs from 27–36 in. above a dining table. Raise the height 3 in. for every additional foot of ceiling height. One or more decorative pendants over a booth will provide bright task light; dimmed for dining, they'll emit a more intimate glow. If you choose a pendant that is open at the bottom, such as a Tiffany-style fixture, make sure the top of the fixture allows some light to escape upward, as well. To eliminate glare underneath, use a diffusing bowl or disk, or a semi-opaque bulb. Also, never use a fixture with an exposed bulb. Be aware that a hanging fixture may also create a harsh glare over a glass table.

Suspended over work islands, chandeliers and pendants are stylish sources of task light for food-preparation chores. Turned up high, these same fixtures may provide sufficient overall illumination for a small kitchen; dimmed they make a decorative kitchen focal point.

OPPOSITE TOP LEFT Oversize pendants make a design statement in this kitchen.

OPPOSITE BOTTOM This offbeat chandelier is a true work of art.

OPPOSITE TOP RIGHT Chrome pendants complement the stainless-steel fixtures and appliances.

ABOVE LEFT A row of delicate crystal pendants adds a jewel-like touch to this kitchen design.

ABOVE RIGHT A custom lighting fixture swoops over this contemporary kitchen.

RIGHT These pendants are set on dimmers for relaxed dining.

track and accent lights

Track lighting is especially helpful in the kitchen. The "track," a surface-mounted channel that holds the lights and brings power to them, can be installed overhead to encompass the general area you want to illuminate. Individual lights can then be attached to the track to shine specifically where you want them and can easily be moved should you revise your lighting plan. Although track lighting was originally introduced into modern kitchens, individual fixtures come in a wide variety of sizes from miniature to major, and in styles from contemporary to traditional. In a modern kitchen, the track system often serves as a design feature, but in more traditional rooms, attention is directed not to the track itself but to what it is lighting. In a modest-size kitchen, tracks can provide both ambient and task illumination, but because they are basically directional, in larger rooms they perform best as task or accent lighting. It's tricky to get track lighting just right. Ask your architect, interior designer, or a lighting specialist for help with the design.

Use accent lighting to call attention to an interesting element or focal point in your kitchen, such as a good-looking range hood, a tile mural above the cooktop, or an exposed brick wall. Sconces, directional track lights, or strip lights can all be employed to accent a decorative feature, and a table lamp might even be used to call attention to a glass front cabinet or armoire.

ABOVE Even if a complete lighting design isn't in your initial budget, install the junction boxes now for future installation.

OPPOSITE TOP LEFT Small spotlights on a shapely track can be focused on work surfaces.

OPPOSITE TOP RIGHT Flying saucer pendants add light, color, and a whimsical feel to this white kitchen.

OPPOSITE BOTTOM LEFT Hanging globe lights add a retro touch to this bold kitchen.

OPPOSITE BOTTOM RIGHT A decorative bronze lantern casts a soft glow against this wall.

resource guide

manufacturers

Above View

4750 South 10th St.
Milwaukee, WI 53221
414-744-7118
www.aboveview.com
Makes ornamental ceiling tiles.

ALNO USA

1 Design Center Pl. #634
Boston, MA 02210
617-896-2700
www.alno.com
European manufacturer of contemporary countertops, storage systems, and cabinetry.

Amana

403 W. 4th St.
Newton, IA 50208
800-843-0304
www.amana.com
Manufactures refrigerators, dishwashers, and cooking appliances.

American Olean Tile Co.

1000 Cannon Ave.
Lansdale, PA 19446-0271
Phone: 215-855-1111
www.americanolean.com
Manufactures ceramic tile.

American Standard

1 Centennial Plaza, P. O. Box 6820
Piscataway, NJ 08855-6820
www.americanstandard-us.com
Manufactures plumbing and tile products.

Armstrong World Industries,

including the divisions of Hartco and Robbins
2500 Columbia Ave.
P.O. Box 3001
Lancaster, PA 17604
800-233-3823
www.armstrong.com
Manufactures floors, cabinets, and ceilings for both home and commercial use.

Artemide

1980 New Hwy.
Farmingdale NY 11735
Phone: 631-694 9292
www.artemide.com
Manufactures lighting fixtures.

Bach Faucets

19701 DaVinci
Lake Forest, CA 92610
866-863-6584
www.bachfaucet.com
Manufactures faucets.

The following list of manufacturers and associations is meant to be a general guide to additional industry and product-related sources. It is not intended as a listing of products and manufacturers represented by the photographs in this book.

Big Chill Refrigerators
877-842-3269
www.bigchillfridge.com
Manufactures retro-style refrigerators.

Blanco America
110 Mount Holly By-Pass
Lumberton, NJ 08048
www.blancoamerica.com
Manufactures sinks and faucets.

Bosch Home Appliances
5551 McFadden Ave.
Huntington Beach, CA 92807
714-901-6600
www.boschappliances.com
Manufactures major and small appliances.

Brewster Wallcovering Co.
67 Pacella Park Dr.
Randolph, MA 02368
781-963-4800
www.brewsterwallcovering.com
Manufactures wallpaper, fabrics, and borders in many patterns and styles.

CaesarStone USA
6840 Hayvenhurst Ave. Suite 100
Van Nuys, CA 91406
818-779-0999
www.caesarstoneus.com
Manufactures quartz-composite countertops.

Corian, a div. of DuPont
Chestnut Run Plaza
721 Maple Run
P.O. Box 80721
Wilmington, DE 19880
800-426-7426
www.corian.com
Manufactures solid-surfacing material for home and commercial kitchens.

Delta Faucet Co.
55 E. 111th St.
P.O. Box 40980
Indianapolis, IN 46280
317-848-1812
www.deltafaucet.com
Manufactures a variety of faucets and finishes for kitchen and bath.

Dex Studios
404-753-0600
www.dexstudios.com
Creates custom concrete sinks and countertops.

Eco Top Surfaces,
a div. of Klip BioTechnologies, LLC
7314 Canyon Rd. E.
Puyallup, WA 98371
253-507-4622
www.kliptech.com
Manufactures eco-friendly countertops made from recycled paper, recycled wood fiber, and plantation grown bamboo fiber.

resource guide

Elkay
2222 Camden Ct.
Oak Brook, IL 60523
630-574-8484
www.elkayusa.com
Manufactures sinks, faucets, and countertops.

Enviro-Trash Concepts
866-671-8878
www.envirotrashconcepts.com
Manufactures an eco-friendly line of trash containment systems.

Fisher and Paykel
5900 Skylab Rd.
Huntington Beach, CA 92647
888-936-7872
www.fisherandpaykel.com
Manufactures kitchen appliances.

Forbo Flooring US
866-Marmoleum
www.forbo.com
Manufactures Marmoleum brand flooring.

Formica Corporation
225 E. 5th St., Ste. 200
Cincinnati, OH 45202
800-367-6422
www.formica.com
Manufactures plastic laminate and solid-surfacing material.

Frigidaire
P.O. Box 212378
Martinez, GA 30917
800-374-4432
www.frigidaire.com
Manufacturers major appliances, including ranges, cooktops, refrigerators, and dishwashers.

General Electric
800-626-2000
www.geappliances.com
Manufactures refrigerators, dishwashers, ovens, and other major appliances.

Glidden
800-454-3336
www.glidden.com
Manufactures paint.

Green Mountain Soapstone Corp.
680 E. Hubbardton Rd.
P.O. Box 807
Castleton, VT 05735
Phone: 802-468-5636
www.greenmountainsoapstone.com
Manufactures soapstone floors, walls, sinks, and countertops.

Haier America
877-337-3639
www.haieramerica.com
Manufactures electronics and appliances, including wine cellars.

Jenn-Air,
a div. of the Maytag Corporation
240 Edwards St.
Cleveland, TN 37311
800-688-1100
www.jennair.com
Manufactures major kitchen appliances including cooktops, ranges, and ovens.

Kemiko Concrete Products
P.O. Box 1109
Leonard, TX 75452-3677
Phone: 903-587-3708
www.kemiko.com
Manufactures acid stains for concrete flooring and other concrete products; creates decorative concrete floors.

Kohler
444 Highland Dr.
Kohler, WI 53044
800-456-4537
www.kohlerco.com
Manufactures kitchen and bath sinks, faucets, and related accessories.

KraftMaid Cabinetry
P.O. Box 1055
Middlefield, OH 44062
888-562-7744
www.kraftmaid.com
Manufactures stock and built-to-order cabinets with a variety of finishes and storage options.

LG
1000 Sylvan Ave.
Englewood Cliffs, NJ 07632
800-243-0000
www.lge.com
Manufactures major appliances.

Lightology
1718 W. Fullerton Ave.
Chicago, IL 60614
866-954-4489
www.lightology.com
Manufactures lighting fixtures.

Maytag Corp.
240 Edwards St.
Cleveland, TN 37311
800-688-9900
www.maytag.com
Manufactures major appliances.

Merillat Industries
5353 W. U.S. 223
Adrian, MI 49221
800-575-8763
www.merillat.com
Manufactures kitchen and bath cabinetry.

Miele
9 Independence Way
Princeton, NJ 08540
800-843-7231
www.miele.com
Manufactures major appliances.

resource guide

MGS Progetti
www.mgsprogetti.com
Manufactures faucets.

Moen
25300 Al Moen Dr.
North Olmsted, OH 44070
800-289-6636
www.moen.com
Manufactures faucets, sinks, and accessories for both kitchen and bath.

Plain and Fancy Custom Cabinetry
Oak St. and Rt. 501
Schaeffertown, PA 17088
800-447-9006
www.plainfancycabinetry.com
Makes custom cabinetry.

Price Pfister, Inc.
19701 Da Vinci
Foothill Ranch, CA 92610
800-732-8238
www.pricepfister.com
Manufactures faucets.

Pyrolave USA
1817 Kenwyck Manor Way
Raleigh, NC 27612
919-788-8953
www.pyrolave.com
Manufactures glazed lava stone countertops.

Rejuvenation
888-401-1900
www.rejuvenation.com
Manufactures kitchen hardware and light fixtures.

Seagull Lighting Products, Inc.
301 W. Washington St.
Riverside, NJ 08075
856-764-0500
www.seagulllighting.com
Manufactures lighting fixtures.

SieMatic-USA
3 Interplex Drive, Ste. 101
Feasterville, PA 19053
215-604-1350
www.siematic.com
Manufactures "fitted" kitchens and kitchen furniture.

Sonoma Cast Stone
P.O. Box 1721
Sonoma, CA 95476
888-807-4234
www.sonomastone.com
Designs and builds concrete sinks and countertops.

Sub-Zero
P.O. Box 44130
Madison, WI 53744-4130
800-222-7820
www.subzero.com
Manufactures refrigerators and freezers in full sizes and as modular drawer-style units.

Vetrazzo
Ford Point, Suite 1400
1414 Harbour Way South
Richmond, CA 94804
510-234-5550
www.vetrazzo.com
Manufactures countertops made of 85 percent recycled glass.

Viking Range Corp.
111 Front St.
Greenwood, MS 38930
888-845-4641
www.vikingrange.com
Manufactures professional-style kitchen appliances.

Watermark Designs, Ltd.
800-842-7277
www.watermark-designs.com
Manufactures faucets and lighting fixtures.

Wilsonart International,
including the division of DeepStar
P.O. Box 6110
Temple, TX 76503-6110
800-433-3222
www.wilsonart.com
Manufactures solid-surfacing materials, plastic laminates, and adhesive for kitchen countertops, cabinets, floors, and fixtures.

Wolf Appliance Company,
a div. of Sub-Zero Freezer Co.
www.wolfappliance.com
Manufactures professional-style cooking appliances.

Wood-Mode Fine Custom Cabinetry
877-635-7500
www.wood-mode.com
Manufactures custom cabinetry for the kitchen.

York Wallcoverings
750 Linden Ave.
York, PA 17405
800-375-9675
www.yorkwall.com
Sells a wide variety of wallpapers and borders; offers on-line decorating tips and advice.

Zodiaq,
a div. of DuPont
800-426-7426
www.zodiaq.com
Manufactures quartz-composite countertops.

associations

National Kitchen and Bath Association (NKBA)
687 Willow Grove St.
Hackettstown, NJ 07840
800-843-6522
www.nkba.org
A national trade organization for kitchen and bath design professionals; offers consumers product information and a referral service.

glossary

Accent lighting: A type of light that highlights an area or object to emphasize that aspect of a room's character.

Accessible design: Design that accommodates persons with physical disabilities.

Adaptable design: Design that can be easily changed to accommodate a person with disabilities.

Ambient light: General illumination that surrounds a room. There is no visible source of the light.

Appliance garage: Countertop storage for small appliances.

Apron: The front panel of a sink that may or may not be exposed.

Awning window: A window with a single framed-glass panel. It is hinged at the top to swing out when it is open.

Backlighting: Illumination coming from a source behind or at the side of an object.

Backsplash: The finish material that covers the wall behind a countertop. The backsplash can be attached to the countertop or separate from it.

Baking center: An area near an oven(s) and a refrigerator that contains a countertop for rolling out dough and storage for baking supplies.

Base cabinet: A cabinet that rests on the floor under a countertop.

Base plan: A map of an existing room that shows detailed measurements and the location of fixtures, appliances, and other permanent elements.

Basin: A shallow sink.

Built-in: A cabinet, shelf, medicine chest, or other storage unit that is recessed into the wall.

Bump out: Living space created by cantilevering the floor and ceiling joists (or adding to a floor slab) and extending the exterior wall of a room.

Butcher block: A counter or table-top material composed of strips of hardwood, often rock maple, laminated together and sealed against moisture.

Casement window: A window that consists of one framed-glass panel that is hinged on the side. It swings outward from the opening at the turn of a crank.

Centerline: The dissecting line through the center of an object, such as a sink.

CFM: An abbreviation that refers to the amount of cubic feet of air that is moved per minute by an exhaust fan.

Chair rail: A decorative wall molding installed midway between the floor and ceiling. Traditionally, chair rails protected walls from damage from chair backs.

Cleanup center: The area of a kitchen where the sink, waste-disposal unit, trash compactor, dishwasher, and related accessories are grouped for easy access and efficient use.

Code: A locally or nationally enforced mandate regarding structural design, materials, plumbing, or electrical systems that states what you can or cannot do when you build or remodel. Codes are intended to protect standards of health, safety, and land use.

Combing: A painting technique that involves using a small device with teeth or grooves over a wet painted surface to create a grained effect.

Cooking center: The kitchen area where the cooktop, oven(s), and food preperation surfaces, appliances, and utensils are grouped.

Countertop: The work surface of a counter, island, or peninsula, usually 36 inches high. Common countertop materials include granite, slate, marble, plastic laminate, and solid-surfacing material.

Cove lights: Lights that reflect upward, sometimes located on top of wall cabinets.

Crown molding: A decorative molding usually installed where the wall and ceiling meet.

Dimmer Switch: A switch that can vary the intensity of the light source that it controls.

Double-hung window: A window that consists of two framed-glass panels that slide open vertically, guided by a metal or wood track.

Downlighting: A lighting technique that illuminates objects or areas from above.

Duct: A tube or passage for venting indoor air to the outside.

Faux painting: Various painting techniques that mimic wood, marble, and other stone.

Fittings: The plumbing devices that transport water to the fixtures. These can include faucets, sprayers, and spouts. Also pertains to hardware and some accessories, such as soap dispensers and instant-water dispensers.

Fixed window: A window that cannot be opened. It is usually a decorative unit, such as a half-round or Palladian-style window.

Fixture: Any fixed part of the structural design, such as sinks.

Fluorescent lamp: An energy-efficient light source made of a tube with an interior phosphorus coating that glows when energized by electricity.

Framed cabinets: Cabinets with a full frame across the face of the cabinet box.

Frameless cabinets: European-style cabinets without a face frame.

Glazing (walls): A technique for applying a thinned, tinted wash of translucent color to a dry undercoat of paint.

Ground-fault circuit interrupter (GFCI): A safety circuit breaker that compares the amount of current entering a receptacle with the amount leaving. If there is a discrepancy of 0.005 volt, the GFCI breaks the circuit in a fraction of a second. GFCIs are required by the National Electrical Code in areas that are subject to dampness.

Grout: A binder and filler applied in the joints between ceramic tile.

Halogen bulb: A bulb filled with halogen gas, a substance that causes the particles of tungsten to be redeposited onto the tungsten filament. This process extends the lamp's life and makes the light whiter and brighter.

Highlight: The lightest tone in a room.

Incandescent lamp: A bulb that contains a conductive filament through which current flows. The current reacts with an inert

glossary

gas inside the bulb, which makes the filament glow.

Intensity: Strength of a color.

Island: A base cabinet and countertop unit that stands independent from walls so that there is access from all four sides.

Kitchen fans: Fans that remove grease, moisture, smoke, and heat from the kitchen.

Lazy Susan: Axis-mounted shelves that revolve. Also called carousel shelves.

Load-bearing wall: A wall that supports a structure's vertical load. Openings in any load-bearing wall must be reinforced to carry the live and dead weight of the structure's load.

Low-voltage lights: Lights that operate on 12 to 50 volts rather than the standard 120 volts used in most homes.

Muntins: Framing members of a window that divide the panes of glass.

Nonbearing wall: An interior wall that provides no structural support for any portion of the house.

Palette: A range of colors that complement one another.

Peninsula: A countertop, with or without a base cabinet, that is connected at one end to a wall or another countertop and extends outward, providing access on three sides.

Proportion: The relationship of one object to another.

Recessed light fixtures: Light fixtures that are installed into ceilings, soffits, or cabinets and are flush with the surrounding area.

Refacing: Replacing the doors and drawers on cabinets and covering the frame with a matching material.

Roof window: A horizontal window that is installed on the roof. Roof windows are ventilating.

Scale: The size of a room or object.

Sconce: A decorative wall bracket, sometimes made of iron or glass, that shields a bulb.

Secondary work center: An area of the kitchen where extra activity is done, such as laundry or baking.

Semicustom cabinets: Cabinets that are available in specific sizes but with a wide variety of options.

Sight line: The natural line of sight the eye travels when looking into or around a room.

Skylight: A framed opening in the roof that admits sunlight into the house. It can be covered with either a flat glass panel or a plastic dome.

Sliding window: Similar to a double-hung window turned on its side. The glass panels slide horizontally.

Snap-in grilles: Ready-made rectangular and diamond-pattern grilles that snap into a window sash and create the look of a true divided-light window.

Solid-surfacing countertop: A countertop material made of acrylic plastic and fine-ground synthetic particles, sometimes made to look like natural stone.

Space reconfiguration: A design term that is used to describe the reallocation of interior space without adding on.

Spout: The tube or pipe from which water gushes out of a faucet.

Stock cabinets: Cabinets that are in stock or available quickly when ordered from a retail outlet.

Subfloor: The flooring applied directly to the floor joists on top of which the finished floor rests.

Task lighting: Lighting designed to illuminate a particular task, such as chopping.

Tone: The degree of lightness or darkness of a color.

Trompe l'oeil: French for "fool the eye." A paint technique that creates a photographically real illusion of space or objects.

True divided-light window: A window composed of multiple glass panes that are divided by and held together by muntins.

Undercabinet light fixtures: Light fixtures that are installed on the undersides of cabinets for task lighting.

Universal design: Products and designs that are easy to use by people of all ages, heights, and varying physical abilities.

Wainscoting: Paneling that extends 36 to 42 inches or so upward from the floor level, over the finished wall surface. It is often finished with a horizontal strip of molding mounted at the proper height and protruding enough to prevent the top of a chair back from touching a wall surface.

Wall cabinet: A cabinet, usually 12 inches deep, that's mounted on the wall a minimum of 15 inches above a countertop.

Xenon bulb: A bulb similar to a halogen bulb, except that it is filled with xenon gas and does not emit ultraviolet (UV) rays. In addition, it is cooler and more energy efficient.

index

index

index

photo credits

Note: DDL=www.davidduncanlivingston.com

page 1: Anne Gummerson, architect: Hammond-Wilson Architects **page 2:** DDL **page 5:** Mark Lohman **page 6:** courtesy of Kraftmaid **pages 8–9:** *left* Olson Photography, LLC, architect: CK Architects; *top right* courtesy of Sub-Zero; *bottom right* DDL **pages 10–11:** courtesy of Armstrong **pages 12–13:** *all* Tony Giammarino/GiammarinoDworkin **pages 14–17:** *all* DDL **page 18:** Anne Gummerson, architect: Joseph Boggs **page 20:** Eric Roth, design: Gregor Cann Design **page 21:** Mark Samu design: Rita Grants **pages 22–23:** *left* DDL; *right* Mark Lohman, architect: Burdge Architects **page 24:** Anne Gummerson, architect: Melville Thomas Architects **page 25:** Tony Giammarino/GiammarinoDworkin **pages 26–27:** *left* Anne Gummerson, architect: HBF+ architects; *right* Tony Giammarino/GiammarinoDworkin **pages 28–29:** *left* courtesy of CaesarStone; *right* Tony Giammarino/GiammarinoDworkin **page 30:** *top* Eric Roth, design: www.benjaminnutter.com; *bottom* DDL **page 31:** *top* Anne Gummerson, design: Brad Creer, Bradford Design; *bottom* Mark Samu, design: Lucianna Samu **page 32:** *top* Tony Giammarino/GiammarinoDworkin; *bottom* DDL **page 33:** Mark Lohman, design: Kathryne Designs **page 34:** DDL **page 35:** *all* DDL **pages 36–37:** *top* courtesy of Kraftmaid; *bottom* courtesy of Armstrong **page 37:** courtesy of Armstrong **pages 38–39:** Anne Gummerson, architect: Joseph Boggs **pages 40–41:** *left and center* Mark Samu, design: Jean Stoffer Design; *top left* Mark Samu, design: Ken Kelly @ Kitchen Designs by Ken Kelly Inc.; *bottom right* Olson Photography, LLC, design: Cucina Designs **page 42:** Tony Giammarino/GiammarinoDworkin **page 43:** DDL **pages 44–45:** *all* Mark Samu, design: Carpen House **pages 46–47:** *clockwise* DDL, Mark Samu design: Jean Stoffer; DDL; DDL; Olson Photography, LLC, design: Ramona Eldridge **pages 48–49:** *all* Eric Roth, design: soaneinterieurs@comcast.net **page 50:** *top and bottom right* Olson Photography, LLC, design: New Canaan Kitchens; *bottom left* DDL **page 51:** Tony Giammarino/GiammarinoDworkin **page 52:** DDL **page 53:** Olson Photography, LLC, design: Shore & Country Kitchens **page 54:** *all* DDL **page 55:** *top* DDL; *bottom* Eric Roth, design: www.decoridesigns.com **pages 56–57:** *all* DDL **pages 58–61:** *all* Tony Giammarino/GiammarinoDworkin **pages 62–63:** *all* DDL **pages 64–65:** DDL **page 66:** *all* DDL **page 67:** *top* Eric Roth, design: www.susansargent.com; *bottom* Tony Giammarino/GiammarinoDworkin **pages 68–69:** *top left* Anne Gummerson, design: Brad Creer, Bradford Design; *bottom left* Mark Samu; *right* Anne Gummerson, design: Eric Liebernecht **pages 70–71:** *left* Olson Photography, LLC, design: Girouard Interiors; *top right* Anne Gummerson, design: Brad Creer, Bradford Design; *bottom right* Olson Photography, LLC, design: Cucina Designs **page 72:** *top left* courtesy of Kitchens by Deane; *top right* courtesy of ALNO; *bottom* courtesy of Kraftmaid **page 73:** *all* Mark Samu, *left* design: Lucianna Samu Design; *right* design: Kitty McCoy, A.I.A. **page 74:** DDL **page 75:** *top left and bottom right* DDL; *top right and bottom left* courtesy of Armstrong **pages 76–77:** *top left* DDL; *top center* Anne Gummerson, architect: Thomas D. Davies; *top right* Mark Samu, design: Lucianna Samu Design; *bottom right and center* DDL **page 78:** *top left and bottom right* Tony Giammarino/GiammarinoDworkin; *top right* courtesy of ALNO; *bottom left* Mark Samu, design: Lucianna Samu Design **page 79:** *clockwise* Anne Gummerson design: Terry Buchanan, Designline; Mark Lohman, design: Andy Marcus; DDL; Mark Lohman; courtesy of ALNO; DDL **page 80:** *top left* courtesy of ALNO; *top right and bottom* DDL **page 81:** DDL **page 82:** *all* Tony Giammarino/GiammarinoDworkin **page 83:** courtesy of Kraftmaid **page 84:** DDL **page 85:** *top* courtesy Armstrong; *bottom right* Mark Lohman, design: Stephanie Hermelee; *bottom left* Mark Samu, design: Lucianna Samu Design **page 86:** *top left* courtesy of Armstrong; *top right* Olson Photography, LLC, design: Clarke Corporation; *right center* DDL; *bottom right* courtesy of ALNO; *bottom left* Olson Photography, LLC, design: Jack Rosen Custom Kitchens **page 87:** *top* courtesy of Plain & Fancy; *bottom* Eric Roth, builder: www.morseconstructions.com **page 88:** Olson Photography, LLC, design: Titus Built **page 90:** Eric Roth, design: www.heatherwells.com **page 91:** DDL **pages 92–93:** Mark Lohman, design: Andy Marcus **pages 94–95:** *clockwise* DDL; courtesy of Armstrong; Olson Photography, LLC, design: Jody Myers-Fierz; Olson Photography, LLC, design: Country Club Homes **page 96:** *all* John Parsekian/CH **page 97:** Eric Roth, design: www.TBAdesigns.com **pages 98–99:** *left* Mark Lohman *right* Eric Roth, design: www.warnercunningham.com **pages 100–101:** *top left* Mark Lohman, design: Will McGaul & Co. *top right* Eric Roth, design: www.christofiinteriors.com; *bottom* Olson Photography, LLC, design: Quaker Road Associates **page 102:** *top* Anne Gummerson, design: Matt Mitchell, architect: Severna Park; *bottom* Eric Roth, design: Tricia McDonagh Interior Design **page 103:** Anne Gummerson, architect: Fred Sieracki **pages 104–105:** *top left* Eric Roth, design: www.horstbuchanan.com; *top right* Olson Photography, LLC, architect: CK Architects; *bottom* Anne Gummerson **page 106:** Eric Roth, design: www.christofiinteriors.com **page 107:** *top left* Mark Lohman, design: Palm Design Group; *top right and bottom* Tony Giammarino/GiammarinoDworkin **pages 108–109:** *top left* Eric Roth, design: Niemtz Design Group; *top right* Olson Photography, LLC, design: Classic Kitchens; *bottom right* Olson Photography, LLC, design: McWilliam-Autore Interiors; *bottom center* Eric Roth, design: www.benjaminnutter.com; *bottom left* Eric Roth **pages 110–111:** *top center* Eric Roth, design: Sebastian Carpenter Design; *top right* Olson Photography, LLC, design: New Canaan Kitchens; *bottom right* Mark Lohman, design: Barclay Butera; *bottom left* Olson Photography, LLC, design: Jody Myers-Fierz **page 112:** *top* Eric Roth, design: www.daliakitchendesign.com; *bottom* Tony Giammarino/GiammarinoDworkin **page 113:** *top* Eric Roth, design: Anthony Catalfano Interiors Incorporated; *bottom* John Parsekian/CH **pages 114–115:** *left* courtesy of Forbo; *top center* courtesy of Armstrong; *top right* Eric Roth, design: www.susansargent.com; *bottom right* courtesy of Armstrong; *bottom left* courtesy of Wilsonart **pages 116–117:** *top and bottom* *left* courtesy of Wilsonart; *bottom right* courtesy of Armstrong **page 118:** Olson Photography, LLC, architect: James Davis Architects **page 119:** *top* DDL; *bottom* courtesy of Armstrong **pages 120–121:** DDL **page 122:** Olson Photography, LLC, design: Clarke Corporation **page 123:** *top right* DDL; *bottom right* Mark Samu, design: SD Atelier AIA; *top left* courtesy of Whirlpool; *bottom left* courtesy of GE **page 124:** Mark Lohman, design: Debbie Nasetta, Roomscapes Inc. **page 125:** *top left and right* courtesy of GE; *bottom* courtesy of Sub-Zero **page 126:** *top* Mark Samu, design: Lucianna Samu Design; *bottom right and center* courtesy of Wolf; *bottom left* courtesy of Sub-Zero **page 127:** *top* courtesy of Sub-Zero; *bottom* Anne Gummerson, design: Dennis and Denise Maksimowitz **pages 128–129:** *top left* Eric Roth, *top right* DDL; *bottom right* Olson Photography, LLC, design: Acorn Cabinetry; *bottom left* Eric Roth, design: www.horstbuchanan.com **pages 130–131:** *top left* Olson Photography, LLC, builder: Ricci Construction Co., Inc.; *top right* Tony Giammarino/Giammarino-Dworkin; *bottom* Mark Lohman, design: Barclay Butera **pages 132–133:** *all* Mark Lohman, *top left* design: Roxanne Packham Design; *top center* design: Stephanie Hermelee & Giulio Kitchen Designs; *bottom* design: Palm Design Group **page 134:** courtesy of Sub-Zero; **page 135:** *top left* courtesy of ALNO; *right and bottom left* courtesy of Sub-Zero **pages 136–137:** *left* Olson Photography, LLC, design: Amazing Spaces; *center and right all* courtesy of Sub-Zero **pages 138–139:** *all* courtesy of Sub-Zero **page 140:** Tony Giammarino/GiammarinoDworkin **page 141:** *top* Eric Roth, design: www.horstbuchanan.com; *bottom* courtesy of ALNO **page 142:** courtesy of Hearst Magazines **page 143:** *top* Mark Samu, design: Ken Kelly @ Kitchen Designs by Ken Kelly Inc. *bottom* courtesy of Enviro-Trash Concepts **page 144:** DDL **page 145:** *left* Mark Samu, design: Donald Billinkoff AIA; *right* courtesy of Whirlpool **pages 146–147:** Mark Samu, design: Ken Kelly@ Kitchen Designs by Ken Kelly Inc. **pages 148–149:** *all* DDL **pages 150–151:** *top left* Mark Samu, design: Artistic Designs by Deidre; *top right* courtesy of Kohler; *bottom right* courtesy of Wilsonart; *bottom left* Mark Samu, design: Andy Levtovsky, A.I.A. **pages 152–153:** *top left* courtesy of Kohler; *top right* Mark Lohman, architect: Michael Lee Architects; *bottom right* Mark Samu, design: Ken Kelly@Kitchen Designs by Ken Kelly Inc.; *bottom left* courtesy of Moen **page 154:** *top left* Mark Lohman, architect: Bill Nicholas; *top right and bottom* courtesy of Kohler **page 155:** *top* courtesy of MGS; *bottom* Olson Photography, LLC, design: Candlelight Cabinetry **pages 156–157:** *center* Mark Lohman, architect: Michael Lee Architects; *all others* courtesy of Kohler **page 158:** Mark Lohman, design: Sue McKeehan **page 159:** *top* courtesy of Kohler; *bottom* Tony Giammarino/GiammarinoDworkin **pages 160–161:** *top left* Mark Lohman, design: Debbie Nasetta, Roomscapes, Inc.; *top right* courtesy of Kohler; *bottom* Mark Lohman, design: Palm Design Group**page 162:** *all* Mark Lohman, *top* design: Janet Lohman & Anne Leeds; *bottom* architect: Burdge Architects **page 163:** *top* Mark Lohman, architect: Michael Lee Architects; *bottom* courtesy of Watermark **page 164:** *top* courtesy of Kohler; *bottom right* Tony Giammarino/GiammarinoDworkin; *bottom left* courtesy of Wood-Mode **page 165:** *top* Mark Samu, architect: Shainberg Architects; *bottom* courtesy of Kohler **page 166:** *top left* courtesy of MGS; *top right* courtesy of ALNO; *bottom* courtesy of Kohler **page 167:** *left* Mark Samu, design: Artistic Designs by Deidre; *right* DDL **page 168:** *top* courtesy of CaesarStone; *bottom all* DDL **page 169:** courtesy of Kohler **page 170:** DDL **page 171:** *clockwise* courtesy of Kohler; Mark Samu, design: Lucianna Samu Design; courtesy of Kohler; Tony Giammarino/GiammarinoDworkin **pages 172–173:** Mark Lohman, design: Ursala Beatt **page 174:** courtesy of SieMatic **page 175:** *all* DDL **page 176:** *top* Tony Giammarino/GiammarinoDworkin; *bottom* courtesy of CaesarStone **page 177:** Olson Photography, LLC, design: Clarke Corporation **page 178:** courtesy of Zodiaq **page 179:** *top* Tony Giammarino/GiammarinoDworkin, *bottom* courtesy of Wilsonart **page 180:** *top* courtesy of SieMatic, *bottom* courtesy of CaesarStone **page 181:** *top* courtesy of Vetrazzo; *bottom* courtesy of Sonoma Cast Stone **pages 182–183:** *top left* Mark Lohman, design: Maraya Droney Design; *center* DDL; *bottom left* Olson Photography, LLC, design: Jack Rosen Custom Kitchens; *bottom right* Olson Photography, LLC, Quaker Road Associates; *top right* courtesy of Ikea **page 184:** courtesy of Deepstar by Wilsonart **page 185:** *top* courtesy of Deepstar by Wilsonart; *bottom* Tony Giammarino/GiammarinoDworkin **page 186:** *top* Mark Lohman, architect: Quentin Parker; *bottom* Tony Giammarino/GiammarinoDworkin **page 187:** DDL **pages 188–189:** *top left* Olson Photography, LLC, design: Brindisi & Yaroscak; *top right* DDL; *bottom right* Olson Photography, LLC, builder: Benchmark Builders; *center* Olson Photography, LLC, architect: Nautilus Architects; *bottom left* Mark Lohman, design: Palm Design Group **pages 190–191:** Eric Roth, architect: Eisen Architects **page 192:** Eric Roth **page 193:** *top* Olson Photography, LLC, architect: Sellars Lathrop Architects; *bottom* Mark Samu **page 194:** Mark Samu, design: Andy Levtovsky, A.I.A. **page 195:** *top left* DDL; *top right* Olson Photography, LLC, design: Candlelight Cabinetry; *bottom* Olson Photography, LLC, builder: Complete Construction **page 196:** Mark Lohman, design: Barclay Butera **page 197:** *top* courtesy of Rejuvenation; *bottom left* Mark Samu, design: BD Design; *bottom right* DDL **page 198–199:** *left, center, and bottom* DDL; *top right* Olson Photography, LLC, **pages 200–201:** *top left* courtesy of Kraftmaid; *top right* DDL; *bottom* Eric Roth **page 202:** *clockwise* Olson Photography, LLC, design: Northeast Cabinet Design; Mark Lohman; Mark Samu, design: Bonacio Construction; DDL; Eric Roth, design: www.heatherwells.com, Eric Roth, design: www.designlabarch.com **page 203:** Mark Samu **pages 204–205:** *top left* Olson Photography, LLC, design: Acorn Cabinetry; *top right* Mark Lohman; *bottom right* Mark Samu, design: Ken Kelly@ Kitchen Designs by Ken Kelly Inc.; *bottom left* Olson Photography, LLC, design: Jack Rosen Custom Kitchens **page 212:** DDL **page 215:** Mark Lohman **page 221:** Eric Roth, design: www.heatherwells.com

If you like

Design Ideas For Kitchens,

take a look at these and other books in the

Design Ideas Series

Design Ideas for Bathrooms
Design inspiration for creating a new and improved bathroom. Over 500 photos.
224 pp.; 8½" x 10⅞"
BOOK #279261

REVISED AND EXPANDED

Design Ideas for Basements
Design solutions for putting your basement space to good use. Over 300 color photos. 208 pp.; 8½" x 10⅞"
BOOK #279424

Design Ideas for Decks & Patios
Design inspiration for creating the deck or patio of your dreams. Over 260 photos.
224 pp.; 8½" x 10⅞"
BOOK #279534

Design Ideas for Concrete & Stone
Covers concrete, granite, marble, travertine, and more. Over 350 photos.
208 pp.; 8½" x 10⅞"
BOOK #279311

Design Ideas for Home Decorating
Design solutions for every room, on every budget. Over 500 photos.
320 pp.; 8½" x 10⅞"
BOOK #279323

Design Ideas for Home Landscaping
Inspiring ideas to achieve stunning effects with landscape. Over 350 photos.
240 pp; 8½" x 10⅞"
BOOK #274154

For more information and to order direct, go to **www.creativehomeowner.com**